To Bill & Bobbie '
Thank you for all
you do for
First Baptist.

Luke 24:31

[signature]

Delivering from Memory

Delivering from Memory

*The Effect of Performance on the
Early Christian Audience*

WILLIAM D. SHIELL

PICKWICK *Publications* · Eugene, Oregon

DELIVERING FROM MEMORY
The Effect of Performance on the Early Christian Audience

Pickwick Publications
An Imprint of Wipf and Stock Publishers
199 W. 8th Ave., Suite 3
Eugene, OR 97401

www.wipfandstock.com

isbn 13: 978-1-60899-678-0

Unless otherwise noted, scripture quotations are from the New Revised Standard Version of the Bible and are copyright © 1989 by the Division of Christian Education of the National Council of the Churches of Christ in the U.S.A. and are used by permission.

Cataloging-in-Publication data:

Shiell, William D.

Delivering from memory : the effect of performance on the early Christian audience / William D. Shiell.

p. ; 23 cm. — Includes bibliographical references and index(es).

ISBN 13: 978-1-60899-678-0

1. Performance. 2. Oral tradition. 3. Memory. 4. Bible. N.T.—Criticism, interpretation, etc. 5. Christian literature, Early—History and criticism. I. Title.

BS2555.52 S52 2011

Manufactured in the U.S.A.

For my son Parker
In celebration of your baptism
Easter 2011

Contents

Preface

THIS PROJECT BEGAN IN McGregor, Texas in 1999. I planned to recite the Sermon on the Mount from memory at First Baptist Church in biblical costume. The day, however, did not go as planned. The music director invited a special guest to perform that morning, and their performance consumed most of the worship hour. I condensed a 25 minute recitation into a rapid 15 minutes. In the process, I learned more about myself than the audience did.

In the years since, I discovered a renewed love for delivery and memory. I spent many days as a child reciting King James English but knew very little of its significance. At Baylor, I studied rhetorical criticism under Mikeal Parsons and ever since had several opportunities to perform the Sermon and many other texts. With each performance, I learn more in the process of preparation; and the audience remarks afterward, "I heard things in performance I never realized before." More recently, something else has happened as well. Following recitations, people tell stories that the performance brings to mind as they listen. Some are related to the narrative; others are ancillary. All are part of what the ancient world broadly called delivery and memory.

Since the publication of *Readings Acts: the Lector and the Early Christian Audience,* the field of performance criticism has emerged in New Testament studies. This book attempts to study early Christian texts from the perspective of ancient delivery and memory for reader and listener. Their performances, much like my experiences, affect reader and hearer. The delivery comes from the memory of the performer and the audience. Both remember as they experience the performance. Both are trained in different ways and are linked together by the experience.

In the same way, this book would not be possible without the attentive listeners in McGregor, San Angelo, and Knoxville who have responded over the years. I am grateful to First Baptist Church for the generous sabbatical leave during the winter of 2010 that gave me time to research the field. Rhonda Ward, Jordan Mallory, and Jonathan Madden have assisted me with the research. Betty Kelley offered Carson-Newman College library's resources throughout sabbatical. Linda Walsh and Kathy Reiko Maxwell offered valuable editorial and theological insights that have shaped this book. I have been thrilled to reunite with my seminary colleague Christopher Spinks on this project. I am so grateful to my wife Kelly and sons Parker and Drake for their support and interest.

My hope is this book continues the discussion that began with ancient performances many years ago. Readers and listeners train each other; as we do, we are delivering from memory.

Abbreviations

1 Clem	*1 Clement*
Aj.	*Ajax*
AJA	*American Journal of Archeology*
AJP	*American Journal of Philology*
Anach.	*Anacharsis*
Ann.	*Annales*
ANRW	*Aufstieg und Niedergang der romischen Welt: Geschichte und Kulture Roms in Spiegel der neuren Forschung.* Edited by H. Temporini and W. Haase. Berlin, 1972—
Ant.	*Antiquities*
Ant. Rom.	*Roman Antiquities*
Apol.	*Apologia*
Apuleius *Metam.*	*Metamorphoses*
Ars	*Ars poetica*
Att. (Cicero)	*Epistulae ad Atticus*
Att. (Nepos)	*Atticus*
Aug	*The Deified Augustus*
BibInt	*Biblical Interpretation*
BTB	*Biblical Theology Bulletin*
Cat.	*In Catalinam*
Cat. Maj.	*Cato Major*
CBQ	*Catholic Biblical Quarterly*

Cher.	*De Cherubim*
Cic.	*Cicero*
CJ	*Classical Journal*
Clu.	*Pro Cluentio*
Col	Colossians
Con.	*Contra Celsum*
Congr.	*De Congressu Quaerendae Eruditionis Gratia*
Conf.	*Confessions*
Contempl.	*De vita contemplativa*
CP	*Classical Philology*
CQ	*Classical Quarterly*
Daphn.	*Daphnis and Chloe*
Dei cogn.	*De dei cognitione (Or. 12)*
Dem.	*Demosthenes*
De Or.	*De Oratore*
Deiot.	*Pro rege Deiotaro*
Det.	*Quod deterius potiori insidari soleat*
Deus	*Quod deus sit immutabilis*
Dial.	*Dialogus de oratoribus*
Div.	*De divinatione*
Ep.	*Epistulae*
Ep. Barn.	Epistle of Barnabas
Epict. disc.	*Discourses of Epictetus*
Eph	Ephesians
Epig.	*Epigrams*
Ep. Ar.	*Letter of Aristides*
Ep. Mor.	*Epistulae Moralia*
Eth. nic.	*Ethica nichomachea*
Fac.	*De facie in orbe lunae*
Flor.	*Florida*
Fam.	*Epistulae ad familiars*
Fronto *ad M. Caes.*	Fronto *ad M. Ceasar*
Gal	Galatians

Glor. Ath.	*De gloria Atheniensium*
Gramm.	*De grammaticism*
Haut.	*Hauton timorumenos*
Hec.	*Hecyra*
Hell.	*Hellenica*
Herm. Mand.	Shepherd of Hermas *Mandates*
Herm. Sim.	Shepherd of Hermas *Similitudes*
Herm. Vis.	Shepherd of Hermas *Visions*
Hipp.	*Hippolytus*
Hist. eccl.	*Ecclesiastical History*
Inst. (Lactantius)	*The Divine Institutes*
Inst. (Quintilian)	*Institutio Oratoria*
Int	*Interpretation*
Inv.	*De inventione rhetorica*
Is. Os.	*De Iside et Osiride*
JBL	*Journal of Biblical Literature*
JEH	*Journal of Evangelical History*
JSNT	*Journal for the Study of the New Testament*
JSNTSup	Journal for the Study of the New Testament: Supplement Series
JSOT	*Journal for the Study of the Old Testament*
JSOTSup	Journal for the Study of the Old Testament: Supplement Series
Jul.	*Divus Julius*
Leg.	*Legum allegoriae*
Let. Arist.	*Letter of Aristeas*
Leuc. Clit.	*Leucippe et Clitophon*
[Lib. ed.]	*De liberis educandis*
LCL	Loeb Classic Library
Macc	Maccabees
Mor.	*Moralia*
Mur.	*Pro Murena*
Mut.	*De mutatione nominum*

Nat.	*Naturalis historia*
Nat. an.	*De natura animalium*
Neot	*Neotestamentica*
NIB	*New Interpreter's Bible*
NovT	*Novum Testamentum*
NTS	*New Testament Studies*
Oed. tyr.	*Oedipus tyrannus*
Or.	*Orator*
Or. Brut.	*Brutus Orator*
Ovid *Metam.*	*Metamorphoses*
Phaed	*Phaedrus*
P.Flor.	*Florilegium Papyrus*
P.Mich.	*Michigan Papyrus*
P.Oslo	*Oslo Papyrus*
P.Oxy.	*Oxyrynchus Papyrus*
Pol. *Phil.*	Polycarp *Letter to the Philippians*
Poet.	*Poetica*
Prob.	*Quod omnis probus liber sit*
Progym.	*Progymnasmata*
Rect. rat. aud.	*De recta ratione audiendi*
QE	*Quaestiones et solutions in Exodium*
Quint. fratr.	*Epistulae ad Quintum fratrem*
Rhet. (Aristotle)	*Rhetorica*
Rhet. Her.	*Rhetorica ad Herennium*
Rosc. Amer.	*Pro Sexto Roscio Amerino*
Sacr.	*De sacrificiis Abelis et Caini*
Sat.	*Satires*
SBL	Society of Biblical Literature
Serv.	*De servis (Or. 10)*
Sest.	*Pro Sestio*
Shep. Vis.	*Shepherd of Hermas Vision*
Sir	Sirach
Somn.	*De somniis*

Strom.	*Stromata*
[Subl.]	*On the Sublime*
TAPA	*Transactions and Proceedings of the American Philological Society*
Ti. C. Gracch.	*Tiberius et Caius Gracchus*
Trad. ap.	*Apostolic Tradition*
Tranq.	*De tranquillitate animi*
Tusc. Disp.	*Tusculan Disputationes*
Ven.	*Venator (Or. 7)*
Vit. beat.	*De vita beata*
Virt.	*De virtutibus*
Virt. (Or. 8)	*De virtute (Or. 8)*
Vit. Plot.	*Vita Plotini*
Vita Virg.	*Life of Virgil*
Vit. Soph.	*Life of the Sophists*
WBC	Word Biblical Commentary
ZNW	*Zeitschrift fur die neutestamentlische Wissenschaft und die Kunde der alteren Kirche*

1

A Performance that Mattered

"I have ridden all the way to this city gate here, not on his back,
but on my ears."

~ Apuleius *Metamorphoses* 1.20–21

IN THE ANCIENT WORLD, a performance affected an audience. Most performers expected the audience to pay attention and participate in the persuasive process. In philosophical and religious groups, the performer and audience identified with communities around moral figures and followed a common pattern set forth in the speech. Performers used biographies to model exemplary behavior in a community and set forth a pattern of living. By repeatedly meeting together and listening to performances, their lives were shaped by the experience. They expected one another to live up to their standard, and they retold the story to each other and to people outside the group. During the performance, they interrupted the speech with questions and dialogue and debated during and after the speech about the topics. The process bonded them and continued the cycle of early transmission of and response to the stories.

The New Testament reflects the oral/aural nature of this kind of communication. Audiences heard readings of sacred texts (Luke 4: Acts 11:15; 2 Tim 3:14; Rev 1:8). Paul even noted the problem of vocal inflection in the transmission between him and the audience (Gal 4:20). Delivery affected the audiences who heard them. People reacted to public speeches negatively (Acts 7) and positively (Acts 2). Reading (Matt 24:15; Mark 13:14; 1 Tim 4:13; 2 *Clem.* 19.1); retaining (*1 Clem.* 35.7–8, 62.3);

memorizing (2 Pet 3:1–9; Herm. *Vis.* 2.1.3–2.2.1); and repeating (2 Tim 3:14) stories and texts became parts of early Christian *paideia* (Heb 12:5–11; Eph 6:4; 2 Tim 2:25, 3:16; Acts 7:22; 22:3; 1 Cor 14:20; 18:3; *1 Clem.* 56.1–16; Pol. *Phil* 4.2; Herm. *Sim.* 6.3.6).

In light of early Christian expectations, what effect does ancient performance have on interpretation? What can be learned about a text's meanings by paying attention to the way a document was likely performed in its late first and early second century settings?

This book proposes that the Greco-Roman rhetorical conventions of delivery and memory can contribute uniquely to performance and interpretation of New Testament texts through reading or preaching in worship or study in classroom. Early Christian audiences expected to see the texts performed using these conventions of delivery and memory. When reading a text in light of these conventions, a preacher, reader, or teacher can imaginatively recapture these conventions in a similar way, engaging performer and audience in a form of early Christian *paideia*.

PERFORMANCE CRITICISM

An emerging discipline in New Testament studies suggests that we can interpret texts in light of the communication event. Performance criticism of the New Testament shows how public delivery of early Christian writings affects interpretation.[1] The text comes alive, an audience is engaged, and they participate in interpreting the document. Several recent monographs and articles explore this concept of contemporary performance as interpretation.[2] Preachers and readers speak the word and perform orally,

1. Rhoads, "Performance Criticism," 118–33 and Rhoads, "Performance Criticism," 164–84. A more recent but condensed versions are, Rhoads, "What is Performance Criticism," in Hearon and Ruge-Jones, *Bible in Ancient Media*, 83–100; and Rhoads, "Performance as Research," 157–98.

2. Three noteworthy books have emerged in the last two years that engage this discipline. See the essays in Childers and Schmit, eds., *Performance in Preaching*; and Cascade's first book in their new series Holly E. Hearon and Ruge-Jones, eds., *The Bible in Ancient and Modern Media*; and Maxwell, *Hearing Between the Lines*. These scholars have indicated that the performance of the texts has a certain interpretive affect on the modern listener. Their creative explorations of performance using theater and drama provide interesting inroads into interpretation. Their analyses draw clues primarily from the text itself or the performer's creativity when a text is presented. However, they largely miss the rhetorical instructions given in the manuals and widely shared by the ancient world and

and the delivery affects interpretation and the formation of community no matter which conventions are used.

This project builds on the previous work of rhetorical criticism of the New Testament. Since George Kennedy,[3] scholars have shown that the New Testament reflects the Hellenistic rhetorical categories: invention, arrangement, style, memory, and delivery. Early Christian writers wrote their works to be delivered orally.[4]

Performance critics study the delivery and reception of Christian writings. Historical events surrounding the early Christian communities affected the listeners in performance.[5] Because of relatively low literacy rates (by Western standards), trained lectors performed and recited texts according to the conventions of delivery and memory.[6] Others told stories privately and publicly to inform and entertain.[7] In turn, audiences responded.

The field of performance criticism from the perspective of ancient rhetoric has already yielded fruitful work. Four are worth noting here because of their importance to this project. Ronald Allen has shown how a preacher can use ancient rhetorical conventions to perform Romans 3 and Mark 13. The Hellenistic diatribe affects a performance of Romans 3. The preacher can demonstrate a dialogue between an imaginary teacher and Paul. Even though silently reading and analyzing the text might reveal the diatribe, a public performance has a certain effect on the speaker's and the audience's interpretation.[8] For example, in Mark 13:31–34, the

the earliest Christian communities. For one notable exception see Allen, "Performance and the New Testament," in Childers and Schmit, 99–116.

3. Kennedy, *New Testament Interpretation*, 3–5.

4. Gamble, *Books and Readers*, 224–26; Botha, "Verbal Art," in Porter and Olbricht, *Rhetoric and the New Testament Essays*, 419; Yaghjian, "Ancient Reading," in Rohrbaugh, *Social Sciences*, 208–9; Graham, *Beyond the Written Word*, 32; Olbricht, "Delivery and Memory," in Porter, *Handbook of Classical Rhetoric*, 159–70; Achtemeier, "*Omne Verbum Sonat*, 17; Quinn, "Poet and Audience," in Haase, *ANRW*, 76–180; Balogh, "*Voces Paginarum*, 84–109, 202–40; Hendrickson "Ancient Reading," 182–96; Shiner, *Proclaiming the Gospel*, 147–51; Shiell, *Reading Acts*, 3.

5. Richard Swanson uses drama, pantomime, and theater to imaginatively construct performance events for contemporary audiences. Swanson, *Provoking Luke*, 1–10.

6. Shiell, *Reading Acts*, 3.

7. Hearon, "Storytelling in the Ancient Mediterranean World," in Thatcher, *Jesus, the Voice, and the Text*, 96–97. Also see Hearon's *The Mary Magdalene Tradition*, 91–93.

8. Allen, "Performance and the New Testament," in Childers and Schmit, *Performance in Preaching*, 109–110.

speaker uses vocal inflection to change the way a listener understands the widow's offering.[9]

Allen's work suggests that a certain kind of understanding occurs in light of the ancient world's performance conventions. The earliest audiences have something to say about the way a text can be interpreted by modern listeners. Therefore, the rhetoric of diatribe and the changes in vocal inflection arise not out of the preacher's preferences but from the world of the first century.

Whitney Shiner shows how Mark builds audience inclusion into the presentation. When a performer uses Greco-Roman rhetorical conventions of gestures, emotions, and memory in performance, an audience experiences delivery in the same way the first performers brought an audience into the story. The Gospel of Mark contains "applause lines," where audiences could interrupt, cheer, and boo. In performance the Gospel includes the audience through direct address and rhetorical questions.[10]

My previous work on gestures and vocal inflection indicates how they play significant roles in a lector's performance of the speeches in Acts. For instance, in Acts 12:17, the NRSV and NIV incorrectly translate the gesture to silence the crowd. In light of Greco-Roman performance conventions, however, the motion is likely a gesture to indicate a defense speech. A trained lector imitates the gestures, facial expression, and emotion in the book of Acts when performing for early Christian audiences.[11]

Kathy Reiko Maxwell has suggested that Luke and Acts contain gaps for a reader and audience to use in performance. The audience becomes a "fellow-worker" in the performance filling the gaps and participating in the experience.[12]

This book goes a step further. Here we want to address how the conventions of delivery and memory affect interpretation. Greco-Roman performances can cause us to raise new questions, interpret texts differently, and hear possible meanings in a written document.

---

9. Allen, "Performance and the New Testament," in Childers and Schmit, *Performance in Preaching*, 114–15.

10. Shiner, *Proclaiming the Gospel*, 192.

11. Shiell, *Reading Acts*, 149.

12. Maxwell, *Hearing Between the Lines*, 3.

THE FUNCTION OF DELIVERY AND MEMORY

This book takes up the Greco-Roman convention of memory as a significant component for the performer and the audience. Hellenistic rhetorical manuals suggest that the performer or lector imitated a text's setting, gestures, and vocal inflection. An orator memorized stories and texts through a process of performance, recitation, visualization, paraphrase, retention, and audience response. The audience came prepared to respond, interrupt, and debate. They remembered as they listened. The performance was a delivery from the memory of reader and listener. This process functioned as instruction or *paideia* for the performer and the audience.

The rhetorical handbooks of Theon (*Progymn.* 66–67, 86.7), Qunitilian (*Inst.* 10.5.19), and pseudo-Cicero (*Rhet. Her.* 3.16.1–3.24.40) indicated that memorization and recitation were critical components in the student's formation. The student memorized, digested, retained, and recited a story for an audience. The practice shaped the character of the student and the audience.[13]

The audience responses not only were included in the story (the story audience), but also were part of the living formation of the community (the performance audience). Reminded of other stories (and texts) from their history that shaped their imagination and lives, the performance audience responded by correcting the speaker and each other. As they responded, they memorized and retained the stories.

For instance, in Apuleius, a storyteller shares a tale rejected by one listener but appreciated by another:

> But his companion, who in stubborn disbelief had rejected his tale from the very start, remarked, "That is the most fabulous fable, the most ridiculous lie that I have ever heard." Then he turned to me: "Now you are a cultured fellow," he said, "as your clothes and manners show. Do you go along with that story?" "Well," I said, "I consider nothing to be impossible. . . But as for Aristomenes, not only do I believe him, by Hercules, but I am also extremely grateful to him for diverting us with a charming and delightful story . . . I have ridden all the way to this city gate here, not on his back, but on my own ears." (*Metamorphoses* 1.20–21)

13. Small, *Wax Tablets of the Mind*, 130.

In Ovid, a listener responds to the story by reminding the storyteller of the elements he omitted (Ovid *Metam.* 12.539) and corrects the speaker with an alternative version (12.540–79).

This process of listening, retaining, correcting, and retelling was part of memorization and formation in a community. Memorization in the ancient world was more than rote repetition of words. The discipline involved paraphrasing; visualizing; participating; remembering; and in some cases, intentionally forgetting to shape the way a story was told. The speaker was given the freedom to elaborate on the text or omit sections depending on the setting or his purpose.

The world of the rhetorical schools, however, was "elitist, sexist, and racist."[14] At best, the elite reading circles and philosophical circles were designed for men with the right patronage. Middle Judaism formed groups to preserve a distinctive Jewish identity around Torah (4 Maccabees 13.22–26).

Early Christian communities entered this same world using rhetorical conventions to subvert the predominant culture and shape new groups around Jesus. Communities were formed in which slave lectors read texts on an equal footing with masters; where Jews and Gentiles shared the same table; and where the stories, narratives, and texts from the first witnesses to Jesus shaped and formed the community. Performing, reciting, and memorizing texts became the early communities' shaping narrative.

This book suggests that the same Hellenistic rhetorical manuals and the audiences of the first and second centuries have something significant to offer to the interpretative process of early Christian performances. We perform texts in light of the eyewitnesses and the communities around them who first heard the stories and texts. These presentations offer "personal connections" within a network of relationships that span 150 years.[15] The use of gestures, vocal inflection, emotion and memory in Christianity's first two centuries can affect how a preacher performs and interprets the text in worship or classroom.

When a text is interpreted in light of the first- and second-century performance event, the contemporary interpreter can respond in the same way that the early Christian audience was shaped and formed by the performance. The ancient world comes into the present and informs

14. Parsons, *Acts*, 21.

15. Bockmuehl, "New Testament Memory," in Barton, Stuckenbruck, and Wold, *Memory in the Bible*, 346–47.

interpretation. Here we are not beginning from the contemporary audience; we are delivering from a memory of the ancient audience contemporary audience. The performer is part of an ongoing dialogue that has been shaped since the first audiences heard these texts recited.

FROM PERFORMANCE TO PAIDEIA

This book suggests that we can broaden interpretation by not only knowing what rhetorical conventions were used, or suggesting that a text could be performed, but also proposing how the performance affected early Christian interpretation. We can raise the following new questions about the text that cannot be deciphered solely through literary analysis: What difference does a performance make, and how is that difference communicated? What choices does a modern performer have in light of the ancient world, and how do I communicate those choices to the audience? How does an audience come better prepared to participate in recollecting and retelling? In light of the first century, what effects will the performance have on groups of listeners? What do the orator and audience remember (and forget) during the performance, and how do they respond?

To address these questions, chapter two describes the importance of Greco-Roman rhetorical conventions of delivery and memory as part of the performance and formation of the performer and the community. In Hellenistic Jewish and Greco-Roman audiences, the performer and the audience were shaped together by the recitation, retention, and response to the performance. The act of memorization was more than the rote verbalization of words. Because of the oral/aural culture, stories and texts could also be retained and recited through paraphrasing (Theon *Progymnasmata* 66–67; Hermogenes *Progymnasmata* 4–6) or by using Pseudo-Cicero's method of memorizing the frame of the story and key points (*Rhet. Her.* 3.16—3.24). All the orators agree that visualization played a key role in retaining and repeating the story. We will see that the performer memorized by using visual clues in the room, using audience members, and "illustrating" the story visually.

An audience's response is more than mere cheers and boos, which are significant in reconstructing the performances but tell us little about the interpretive effect on the community. We will see that in some cases, the practice of storytelling is met with such audience responses, as telling another story, correcting the story previously read, or correcting each other about their memories. The effect of these multi-layered responses indicates an engaged community formed and shaped by collective memories and responses to a story. When recounting narratives, readers could manipulate the moods and emotions of the audience using the emotions in the text. When the audience in the story (the story audience) responded emotionally, the audience in performance (the performance audience) can have the opposite response (Aristotle *Rhetor.* 2.8.1386a). Another powerful effect on the audience involved not only what a speaker put into the retelling but also what he omitted (Philo *Cher.* 30.102; *Congr.* 8.39–40). In the process, the ancient speaker and listener were affected, shaped, and formed. The process, however, involved memorization, paraphrase, repetition, and transmission of these stories and texts.

Chapter three will propose how these conventions can be seen in early Christian documents. The New Testament books functioned as charter documents to provide formation around Jesus and shape the character of early Christ-followers into imitators of one another and of him.[16] Prior to performance, the reader practices, remembers, retains, and paraphrases the reading. During performance, the lector remembers *testimonia*, omits information, elaborates a saying, and responds to the audience. An audience responds with memories of other stories and reacts to the speaker's performance. The entire process shapes early Christian *paideia*.

Early Christian texts contain audience reactions, which we call the story audience. The reader anticipates reaction and change in the performance audience. Sometimes the performance audience mirrors the story audience. At other times, the opposite can happen. We will examine instances of both. We will note that performances as they are described in early Christian texts (the story audience) through the fourth century C.E. and examine the likely outcome of these performances in communities (the performance audience). Performance, text, memory, and audience come together in early Christian *paideia* literature. The performances of early Christian writings included readings, responses, memory, and the early communities' formation.

In chapter four, I will propose a set of questions based on the conventions of ancient delivery where one can read and listen with the

---

16. Parsons, *Acts*, 21.

eyes of the ancient performers and auditors. If you can discover the clues structurally in the narrative and establish how the text shows the rhetorical conventions, then one can look for performance conventions that guide interpretation.

We will look for test cases where an interpreter can bring the previous information to bear on a performance of Jesus. Instead of just viewing Jesus from one angle of the writer or the presuppositions of the interpreter, performers had several options at their disposal in performance, depending on the need of the audience. These examples from the Synoptics open possibilities for performance and interpretation of the central figure of Christian *paideia*, Jesus. Not all texts are shaped by a performance, but certainly all texts were performed and can be. For certain ones, however, performance changes or modifies how one reads a text. Here I am not suggesting that a performance satisfies all questions of interpretation or offers conclusions to puzzling problems. This kind of performance analysis raises different kinds of questions about interpretation. Instead of first asking how a modern audience responds to a performance, this analysis begins with the ancient performance and suggests that these performance conventions should shape how we deliver to a modern audience.

In light of the ancient audience, the performance can shape a contemporary community's interpretation, especially in the place where most people hear these texts read, in worship or classroom. This communication event comes together most frequently for modern listeners in the classroom and in public worship. This three-part performance event requires the performer (preacher or lector) who has memorized and retained the story, an engaged audience, and the text itself. In chapter five, we will draw conclusions connecting the ancient audience to modern interpretation. If we read and perform in light of the ancient audience, how does that shape *paideia* of the listener and reader?

Based on the conventions of ancient delivery, we read the story audience and imagine the effect on the performance audience. Here one can read and listen with the eyes of the ancient performers and auditors. If an interpreter can discover the structural clues in the narrative and establish how the text shows the rhetorical conventions, then she can look for performance conventions that guide interpretation. This method involves analysis, visualization, recall, practice, paraphrase, audience preparation, performance, and response.

Reading early Christian texts is an interpretive act. For ancient audiences, the performances opened a variety of options for listeners then and now. In so doing, the performance shaped the community.

2

Delivery and Memory in the Ancient World

"The ears of the city, therefore, we found hungry for this varied type of oratory."

~ Cicero *Brutus Orator* 30.106

IN THE ANCIENT WORLD, the five classic components for planning and delivering speeches were invention, arrangement, style, memory, and delivery. Invention prepared the speech. Arrangement organized the parts. Style included various figures, tropes, and words used to compose the speech. Memory and delivery retained the words and performed them publicly.

A survey of the rhetorical manuals, Hellenistic Jewish texts, and records of performances reveal the significance to the process of memory and delivery in the culture. Learning and delivery trained the orator in the values and characteristics of the Roman world, or in the case of the variety of forms of Judaism, the habits of Jewish practices. Memory and delivery proved to be more than the end of a process but the outcome of a good student. By participating in a rhetorical school or philosophical circle, the student was a part of the audience. He was shaped by the experience and learned to shape others in performance.

The audience played a significant role in the formation of the orator. Ancient audiences who lacked access to written texts, unlike modern Westerners, listened from their memories. They retold, corrected, admonished, applauded, and in some circles participated in the editing process as part of a reading circle called the *amici*. Without access to written manuscripts and widespread libraries, their collective recall formed and shaped the performance as much as the performer. The reader delivered from the auditors' memories as much as his own.

To set the stage for understanding early Christian texts, we need to get into this world of the performance of ancient documents prior to and around the first three centuries C.E. Here we catch a glimpse of the world of memory and delivery. The definition of memory will be broadened beyond rote memorization. Memory was a process of learning, recall, paraphrase, retention, practice, and behavior modification.

In delivery, we will see the ongoing collaboration between reader and audience and note that the audience is shaped by the performance itself to emulate a person's values in the ancient world. In some cases, communities of people could identify with a model figure. The act of reading included them in the communities. People learned from one another and modeled behavior patterns for each other through reading and performance.

DELIVERY BY THE PERFORMER

According to Cicero, when Demosthenes was asked for the most important aspect of rhetoric, he answered with three words: "Delivery, delivery, delivery." (*De Or.* 3.213; *Or. Brut.* 56). In a speech, many choices had to be made; for the performer and the audience, some elements affected the audience more than others. These were the body, the rhetorical figures, and the performer's use of memory.

The Body

Gestures

Instructions for gestures are found throughout ancient manuals and speeches. For example, Quintilian identifies 24 hand and arms gestures to use for various settings for delivery and parts of speeches. The orator uses the gestures to maintain good rhythm (Cic. *Brut.* 80.278), mark sections in a speech (11.3.92), alert the audience (Quin. *Inst.* 11.3.98), and communicate nonverbally (Cicero *De Or.* 3.214).

A speech's success, however, is judged by the emotional effect on the audience and the reaction of the crowd (Cicero *De Or.* 2.178; 2.188; 3.216; Quint. *Inst.* 6.1.30). As long as speakers do not perform effeminately, the recitations fulfill expectations. (*Or. Brut.* 17.59–60). Good speakers plan their gestures prior to delivery and play their audience like strings on a lyre (Cicero *De Or.* 3.216; *Or. Brut.* 69). Orators use gestures for surprise, indignation, entreaty, anger, adoration, reproach, grief, insistence, emphasis, laughter, irony, and aversion (*Inst.* 11.3.92–102; *Rhet. Her.* 3.11–15).[1]

Face

The face plays an important role in conveying the "feelings of the mind" (Cicero *De Or.* 3.58.223). Quintilian notes that the greatest influence the speaker has is a glance. The eyes show threats, flattery, sorrow, joy, pride, or submission (*Inst.* 11.3.72–73). The same can be said for the gaze. A speaker often fixes his attention on the crowd or a judge in self-defense,[2] to single out himself, or to disarm the crowd with humor (Fronto *ad M. Caes.* 3.6; Cicero *De Or.* 2.55.225; Tacitus *Ann.* 2.37–38).

Voice

Speakers and audience rely on the voice for delivery and appeal to the Muses for help (Homer *Iliad* 484–493, 761–762; 11.218–220; 14.508–510). The text provides necessary guidance for delivery of vocal inflection; but oral and written styles differ, as Aristotle notes. The verbal has a dramatic flair (Aristotle *Rhet.* 3.12.1 1413b).

To prepare, the reader starts with the emotions in the text. Based on the emotions described, the voice modifies and changes accordingly. Dionysius notes, "Here the words themselves show what kind of delivery is needed for them" (*Dem.* 54). As a speech becomes more intense, the speaker changes his vocal intensity. When a character anticipates death, faces an unexpected outcome, or uses a sudden turn of phrase, the speaker uses an ironic tone (Sophocles *Ant.* 31; Plato *Apol.* 24b5; Xenophon *Hell.* 2.3.24). The audience can react with humor or surprise.[3]

---

1 For a complete list of gestures with visual representation see my book *Reading Acts: the Lector and the Early Christian Audience*, 63–78.

2. Anderson, *Second Sophistic*, 66.

3. Boegehold, *When a Gesture was Expected*, 101.

Depending on the settings and the issues in their speeches, students are trained to vary their emotions, including anger, compassion, fear, energy, joy, and dejection (Cicero *Or. Brut.* 17.56–59). Humor is appropriate in every situation and style. An orator uses something as simple as an ironic turn of phrase or a more theatrical characterization called an *ethopeia* (see below), where an orator imitates a stock figures who people mock in society (Cicero *Pro Clu.* 68–69).

Four emotions are connected to character formation: pity, indignation, envy, and zeal or emulation. The orator evokes these from the audience, connecting them to the life of a virtuous figure in performance.[4] Depending on how the orator uses emotions, they can have the opposite effect on the audience. To calm an audience, orators "put hearers in the corresponding frame of mind, and represent those with whom they are angry as formidable, or as worthy of reverence, or as benefactors, or as involuntary agents, or as much distressed at what they have done" (Aristotle *Rhet.* 2.5.15 1383a [George A. Kennedy]). For instance, fear in a scene has a positive effect on the audience as opposed to hopelessness, according to Aristotle. Instead of people becoming more afraid, a portrayal of fear in performance actually prompts them to think that "something can be done." When the audience needs to feel that they are in some sort of imminent danger,

> He should make them realize that they are liable to suffering; for [he can say that] others even greater [than they] have suffered, and he should show that there are others like them suffering [now] (or who have suffered) and at the hands of those from whom they did not expect it and suffering things [they did not expect] and at a time when they were not thinking of [the possibility] (Aristotle *Rhet.* 2.5.15 1383a [George A. Kennedy]).

To inspire confidence, the performer creates the impression that safety is near or the audience is in the presence of someone who inspires confidence or prevents harm. (*Rhet.* 2.5.1383a.15). In the face of danger, an audience becomes confident when the characters face unique experiences for the first time or have the resources to handle danger and seem to have the means to deal with the problem. For instance, in the performance of inexperienced sailors in a storm, the audience's confidence or sense of

---

4. Aristotle on fear and pity in *Rhet.* 2.5.1–15 1382a-1383a and 2.8.1–15 1385b-1386b; Cicero *de Or.* 2.211 and Quint 6.2.34. The emotions of the orator are taken over— Cic. *De Or.* 2.189–190 and Quint *Inst.* 6.2.3; 6.2.26–36.

calm grows even if the characters face danger. They are likely to be more confident even if the characters have never been at sea in a storm as much as when they have the experience and resources to deal with the storm. In both cases, their confidence can grow by watching and participating in the performance (*Rhet.* 2.5.18.1383a–b).

Aristotle mentions other sources of confidence when the listener compares himself to others in the story. Confidence grows if the audience has conquered weaker or stronger people. A listener grows confident if he thinks he is wealthier than a rival in the story, is physically strong, owns extensive territory, or possesses weapons of war. They can also feel confident if they have wronged no one. They can become angry and then confident if they know that they are the one who has been wronged and that a "divine power" is on the side of those who have been wronged. If the audience believes that they will not fail or succeed completely, depending on the circumstances, their anger and confidence can change with the emotion in the performer's voice (*Rhet.* 2.5.19—20.1383b).

Rhetorical Figures

Along with bodily and vocal choices, rhetorical figures have a tremendous effect on the audience. Thus, we turn from the discussion of the movement and actions of the performer to elements found within the text that a performer could exploit. I have selected a few such figures in ancient rhetoric that will also play prominently in our discussion of early Christian texts: lists, riddles, fables, visualization, and characterizations.

Lists

The performer employs two kinds of lists, catalogues and *sorites*. Catalogues of names, cities, and ships arouse the expectation and anticipation of the audience. These lists play a significant role in performing poetry and *encomia* (praise). They are an exercise in mnemonic technique, and the crowd reacted to the orator's skill. The performance creates expectancy and urgency in the audience. Homer arouses their urgency to prepare listeners for a battle scene or a contest with long list catalogues often during the description of the speech. (*Iliad* 7.162–168; 8.261–267; 12.88–104; 23.288–351, 754–756, 836–838. *Odyssey* 8.111–119). To a modern audience, this might seem like a bit of an intrusion. For the performer, this technique functions as part of an encomium of praise. In

the Iliad, Homer praises Agamemnon with an encomium prior to listing
the ships (Quint. *Inst.* 2.7.10–13; Homer *Iliad* 2.477–493) and describes
battle scenes with long lists (*Iliad* 5.677–678; 16.415–418; 21.209–210).

The performance audience is impressed in two ways. The arrangement of the parts delight the audience, and the speaker's ability to perform the piece impresses them and binds the listeners to the contents
of the list. According to Minchin, "The sustained and therefore exciting
nature of such a performance will be a compound of interest, delight,
admiration, and excitement. This will act as a kind of charm which will
bind them to the list."[5]

The second list, the *sorites,* links virtues and vices in performance.
Sorites are usually words, enthymemes, or concepts that build on each
other like links in a chain. Commonly called the "chain link effect" or *gra-
datio* in ancient rhetoric, these are used in wisdom literature and ancient
rhetoric to explain the origins and development of either virtue or vice
(Philo *Sacrif. Abel.* 27; Philo *Leg. Alleg.* 1.64; Wis. 8.7; 1QS 4.2–6; Wis.
6.17–20). One example from Cicero explains the roots of wickedness.

> As you could not find every kind of crop, or tree on every soil,
> so every kind of life does not produce every evil deed. The city
> creates luxury, from which avarice inevitably springs, while from
> avarice audacity breaks forth, the source of all crimes and mis-
> deeds. On the other hand, this country life, which you call boor-
> ish, teaches thrift, carefulness, and justice. (Cicero *Rosc. Amer.*
> 27.75 [Freese, LCL])

Riddles

To achieve a sense of liveliness, surprise, and delight, as well as allow the
hearer to instruct himself, the orator uses metaphors, hidden meanings,
and riddles (Aristotle *Rhet.* 3.2.5 1405b). Hidden meanings in performance affect the listener as well by leaving something for the hearer to
discover (Quintilian *Inst.* 9.2.65):

> For thus the judge will be led to seek out the secret which he would
> not perhaps believe if he heard it openly stated, and to believe in
> that which he thinks he has found out for himself. In doing this

5. Minchin, "Performance of Lists," in Worthington, *Voice into Text,* 19. In describing the battles of the Iliad, Homer includes lists such as the catalogue of Ships in *Iliad*
14.315–327 to "arouse in the audience expectations of a great story" (5.677–678; 16.415–
418; 21.209–210), 17–18.

we shall find emotional appeals, hesitation and words broken by
silences most effective. (*Inst.* 9.2.71 [Butler, LCL]).

The images in the metaphors and riddles are placed before the audience's
eyes, creating liveliness and surprise (Aristotle *Rhet.* 3.11.1–3) as the
listener discovers the meaning. Even though Quintilian warns against
excessive use of riddles, veiled meanings and metaphors, their presence
suggests another way to involve the audience in the mystery.

Fables

Aristotle describes two kinds of parables used in rhetoric, closely related
to examples, factual and invented (*Rhet.* 2.20.1 1393b). Allegories (*Rhet.*
8.6.58) and fables (Theon *Progymnasmata* 74) are often told with a certain sense of obscurity and can achieve the same kind of effect as riddles.
They are most effective when used to draw analogies and metaphors from
occurrences readily seen in life (*Inst.* 5.11.22–30). They cause their listeners to seek out the hidden meaning and in turn receive instruction. In
speeches, they give an "image of truth" and are taught in the rhetorical
schools to be used in various ways for narrative, refutation, and confirma-
tion (Theon *Progym.* 76).

    In Jewish literature, apocalypses use allegory to keep their secrets
from the uninformed and to encourage those who are facing persecution
(4 Ezra 9.16–19). Philo uses Jewish historical examples allegorically for a
variety of purposes depending on the context.[6]

Visualization

Visualization, or *ekphrasis,* portrays images "clearly before the sight" of
the audience (Theon *Progymnasmata* 118 [Kennedy, 45]). This figure
produces *enargeia* or vividness with emotion (*pathos*) and excitement
(*kinesis*)[7] because the images correspond to what is practical or truthful
(Aristotle *Rhet.* 3.11.1411b.20).

---

  6 Alexandre, "Rhetorical Argumentation in Philo," in Caquot, Hadas-Lebel, and
Riaud, *Hellenica et Judaica,* 25–26. Interestingly for the purposes of this project, he used
the meaning of the names of Joseph's sons as allegories for the different components of
memory. Simeon was the listener, Manasseh was recollection, almost forgetful. Reuben
"the seeing son" was the one with a "good disposition," Ephraim's name meant "memory,"
and he had the most complete memory of all. Philo *Congr* 8.39–40; *Mut.* 16.97

  7. Webb, "Imagination and Emotions," in Braund and Gill, *Passions in Roman
Thought,* 118.

To prepare, the speaker immerses himself in the text's images and words so that they are delivered in performance with the same emotions used by the character in the text.[8] During performance, a speaker can arouse pity, indignation, or misery with vivid accounts (Cicero *De inv.* 1.54.104). This creates surprise or fear, "transcending the audience's sense of what is credible" (Longinus *[Subl.]* 15.8).

In Ovid, the listener sees images including his wife, city, and events of his past (*Tristia* 3.4.55–60; *Ex Ponto* 1.8.33–38). He is able to "transcend his condition" in exile, but the images cause even greater stress "precisely because they remind him of his physical separation."[9]

Characterization

Readers impersonate people through speeches in character (*prosōpopoiia*) or imitation of a figure in a story or speech (*ethopeia*) (Cicero *Pro Caelio* 33–36; *Pro Milo* 36). The characterizations vary depending on the individual's age and mannerisms (*Poetics* 1448a 2.1–14). Students are trained and admonished to perform the work and keep their personal emotions in balance as the student imitated the individual (Suet. *Gram.* 4; Theon *Progymnasmata* 105; Plut. *Adol. Poet. Aud.* 25–26).

A simple method is found in Theon:

> One should have in mind what the personality of the speaker is like, and to whom the speech is addressed: the speaker's age, the occasion, the place, the social status of the speaker; also the general subject which the projected speeches are going to discuss . . . Different ways of speaking belong to different ages of life, not the same to an older man and a younger one; the speech of a younger man will be mingled with simplicity and modesty, that of an older man with knowledge and experience. Different ways of speaking would also be fitting by nature for a woman and for a man and by status for a slave and a freed man, and by activities for a soldier and farmer, and by state of mind for a lover and a temperate man (*Progymnasmata* 115–116 [Kennedy]).

These personality traits are especially important in recitation. They provide a script for the reader to copy. As a speaker reads the text, he uses the same gestures as if he does not have a script. (Cornelius Nepos *Atticus* 4.2; Dionysius of Halicarnassus *Dem.* 53). Dionysius connects style of writing,

8. Ibid., 120.

9. Ibid., 117.

oratory, and recitation. They match their gestures, facial expressions, and vocal inflection.

The schools train orators to use *ethopeia* and *prosōpopoiia* mimicry and imitation to evoke an emotional response from an audience. Just as the orator and lector use the emotions of pity, indignation, envy, and zeal in his voice, so these are also reflected in his characterizations and imitations of people in the text.

If the orator expresses emotion toward the characters, the audience is able to identify with the same emotions. (Cic. *De Or.* 2.190–198; *Rhet. Her.* 2.50). An orator manipulates the emotions especially if he does not easily identify with the character. In contrast, if the character is someone the audience should pity, the speaker presents him through the eyes of a person pitying him. (Aristotle *Poet.* 1452b28—1453a22; Aristotle *Eth. nic.* 1106b21–3).[10]

When a character experiences undeserved suffering, a performance evokes pity from the audience.[11]

> They pity their acquaintances, unless they are very closely connected to their household, and in that case they feel for them as they feel about their own future suffering; this is why Amasis, according to reports, did not weep when his son was led off to death but did [weep] for a friend reduced to begging; for the latter was pitiable, the former dreadful; for the dreadful is something different from the pitiable and capable of expelling pity and often useful to the opponent; for people no longer pity when something dreadful is near themselves. And they pity those like themselves in age, in character, in habits, in rank, in birth; for in all these cases something seems more to apply to the self; for in general, one should grasp here, too, that people pity things happening to others insofar as they fear for themselves. And since sufferings are pitiable when they appear near at hand and since people do not feel pity, or not in the same way, about things ten thousand years in the past or future, neither anticipating nor remembering them, necessarily those are more pitiable who contribute to the effect by gestures and cries and display of feelings and generally in their acting [*hypokrisis*]; for they make the evil seem near by making it appear before the eyes either as something about to happen or as something that has happened, and things are more pitiable when

10. Levene, "Pity, Fear, and the Historical Audience," in Braund and Gill, *Passions in Roman Thought*, 133.

11. Ibid., 131.

just having happened or going to happen in a short space of time. For this reason signs and actions [contribute to pity]; for example, the clothes of those who have suffered and any such things, and words and any other such things of those in suffering; for example, of those on their deathbed; for all such things, through their appearing near, make pity greater. And most pitiable is for good people to be in such extremities, since one who is unworthy [is suffering] and the suffering is evident before our eyes. (*Rhetoric*, 2.8.12–15.1386a [Kennedy])

As mentioned previously, humor plays an important role in portraying people as stock characters in a play. Cicero uses the playwright Terence's practice of *ethopeia* to potray characters with rapid bodily movement,[12] and language that causes the audience to laugh. The most popular are the arrogant, proud, thieves, or swindlers. (Cicero *Clu.* 68–69).

When a character is being accused or questioned, raillery evokes laughter from the audience. Raillery is a one or two line retort that uses an ironic tone of voice, setting the questioner back and amusing the audience (2.54.218, 220). Harsh tones evoke even more laughter from the audience because the face and voice create a different reaction than the delivery style. (Cicero *De Or.* 2.55.225; 2.71.289).

Memory

For a speaker or reader, memory work is a part of Greek, Roman, and rabbinic education in preparation for a public life in oral culture. (Plato *Prot.* 325E; *Leg.* 7.810E-811A; Cicero, *Tusc. Disp.* 2.27; Josephus *Apion* 2.171–183; *Life* 12–13).[13] Memory involves planning the delivery of the speech, retention of the material, adjustments to the audience during performance, and paraphrases of other materials.

Greeks and Romans do not have an equivalent expression for "to memorize"[14] nor did the concept of memorization involve only rote memory. Instead they use various expressions and practices to describe the experience. They share the word *ekmanthanō* and *edisco*, respectively, "to learn thoroughly."[15] Greek literature associates memory with the phrase "from the mouth." This phrase occurs in two forms in Greek, *apo*

12. Richlin, "Gender and Rhetoric," in Dominik, *Roman Eloquence*, 95.
13. Flavius Josephus, *Life* 12–13 (Mason, Flavius Josephus), 12.
14. Small, *Wax Tablets*, 134.
15. Ibid., 133.

stomatos or *apostomatizō*, when describing the act of memory (Homer *Odyssey* 12.187; Plato *Thaetetus* 143a; Xenophon *Symposium* 3.5–6). Latin literature prefers the expression *ad verbum*, literally "to the word," not "verbatim." Hellenistic Jews prefer "the remembrance [tablets] of the heart" in association with memory (2 *Bar.* 50.1; Prov. 3.1–3; 7.3 LXX) and the rhetorical connection to one of the bodily organs associated with speech, retelling, and memory. In all cases, memory is not a separate part of the brain but is placed in various organs of the body.[16]

The literature of memory, much like the fluid language to describe it, reflects a process of retention and learning rather than a static act of rote memorization. Memory is a process of practice, retention, recall, forget-fulness, and performance. This process begins when a reader prepares his mind to retain information. This creates a foundation of knowledge, like the foundation of a person's house (Philo *Cher.* 30.102) leading to learn-ing, recalling information, remembering, and retaining (Plato *Meno* 81d; Aristotle *Rhet.* 1250a35).

Speech is considered the "brother of the intellect." (Philo *Det.* 12.40). Much like a cistern for a camel, memory serves as the water for life (44.146). Out of knowledge, recall, learning, and attentiveness rises memory (Philo *Cher.* 30.102). Two signs of an effective memory are a fruitful life (*Mut.* 16.97) and a vivid imagination. When a person enjoys someone's presence in his mind's eye (Aristotle *Rhet.* 1.11.1370b.20) or mentally bridges a gulf between past and present, a person is re-membering effectively (Aristides "A Letter to the Emperors Concerning Smyrna" 19.2–3).

The enemy of memory is forgetfulness. Once the heart receives an impression, forgetfulness either smoothes or dulls the edges of the im-pression. (Philo *Deus* 9.43). To fight the problem of forgetfulness, a per-son practices recollection (Philo *Congr.* 8.39–40).

Schools train orators and lectors to plan and remember their speech-es ahead of time using a system of visualization and reconstruction (*Rhet. Her.* 3.16–24; Cicero *De or.* 3.221; Quint. *Inst.* 11.2.40–44). They consider the heart and mind to be made of wax, ready to be impressed with images, words, and thoughts (Quint. *Inst.* 11.2.10–13; 11.2.34; Prov. 3.1–4 LXX).

To shape and impress the wax, students visualize a speech much like an architect designs a room or a mapmaker plans a city. Orators spend

---

16. Ibid., 136.

time creating a series of images and backgrounds in the mind where they can file words and objects to represent the words to retain. Preparing these mental palaces or storage places to put information are just as much a part of memory work as the information and delivery itself. The orator practices with these images and backgrounds as much as the speech. Just as an athlete in a gym trains for sports, the orator trains the mind to retain words. They practice repeatedly to form impressions on the mind (Quint. *Inst.* 11.2.10–13; 11.2.34) like wax on an ancient tablet. The location on the tablet forms mental impressions (Prov. 3.1–4 LXX; *Rhet. Her.* 3.16–24), and over time, the mind matures and ripens.

For instance, a speaker remembers the layout of a room and the people in it by using an already preconceived imaginary room. The orator has already chosen a room's layout as a mental image in which to place things in his heart. When he sees the people sitting in the room, he places them on the image that he has on the heart. The people leave an impression on the "tablets of the heart." A speaker develops a personal system of symbols to connect ideas in his mind, leading the memory from one idea to the next (Quint. *Inst.* 11.2.30).

Memorization encompasses the entire process that involves filing away items in the memory bank, repetitively practicing, and visualizing the speaking event. Quintilian considers recollection one of the most important parts of memory because each person's recall ability grows over time (Quint. *Inst.* 11.2.43; *Rhet. Her.* 3.24). A person who struggles to remember others' speeches is considered to have a slow heart or a slow memory (Quint. *Inst.* 11.2.4; 11.2.29–35).

Because of the oral/aural culture, stories and texts are also retained and recited through paraphrase (Theon *Progymnasmata* 66–67; Hermogenes *Progymnasmata* 4–6). School traditions are handed down, remembered, paraphrased, and repeated (Seneca *Ep.* 33.4). Selections of Hebrew scriptures and religious texts are memorized as *testimonia* (2 Macc. 2.25; Quintilian *Inst.* 5.11.37–44). Famous sayings and events are remembered in the form of *chreia*, expanded with examples, and paraphrased with practice (Theon *Progymasmata* 3).

In performance a "memorized speech" took several forms. The speaker keeps the major thoughts, changes a phrase or two by adding new words, drops a few words from the original, or substitutes an original word for another (Quint. *Inst.* 11.2.48). They memorize the frame of the story and key points (*Rhet. Her.* 3.16–3.24) but adapt the speech in delivery. They paraphrase themes that need a "good restatement." Theon suggests, "Begin with the simplest, thing, for example, with exercise of memory, then pass to paraphrasing some argument in a speech, either the prooemion or narration." (Theon *Progymasmata* 109P [Kennedy]). Orators memorize (Eunapios *Vit. Soph.* 2.8) and paraphrase their speeches as well as others', much like sculptors recasting a piece of art with wax (Quint. *Inst.* 10.5.10–11).

Through a paraphrase, a speaker overcomes gaps and interruptions in delivery. Speakers are free to adapt and speak at will to avoid stumbling through sections they cannot remember verbatim (Quint. *Inst.* 11.2.48), to anticipate exchanges from the audience, and to return to a theme when the audience interrupts him.[17]

> We have to study actors as well as orators, that bad practice may not lead us into some inelegant or ugly habit. The memory too must be trained carefully learning by heart as many pieces as possible both from our Latin writers and the foreigner. (Cicero *De* or. 1.34.156 [Sutton, LCL])

ROLES OF THE AUDIENCE

Much like the orator or lector, the audience does more than simply fill a space in the room. They are part of the process through listening, responding, and remembering. A lector "reads to the ears" of the audience, and the effect is so powerful "the hearers and the word [come] together without any separation between them" (Philo *QE* 2.34).

Listen

The audience's first role was listening. Philo expressed this function best when he said,

> Hardly a day passes but the lecture-halls and theatres are filled with philosophers discoursing at length, stringing together without stopping to take breath their disquisitions on virtue. Yet what profit is there in their talk? For instead of attending, the audience dismisses their minds elsewhither, some occupied with thoughts of voyaging and trading, some with their farming and its returns,

17. Hadot, *Ancient Philosophy*, 151–52.

others with honours and particular trade and business, others with
the vengeance they hope to wreak on their enemies, others with
the enjoyments of their amorous passions, the class of thought in
fact differing with the class of person. Thus, as far as what is being
demonstrated is concerned, they are deaf, and they are present in
the body and absent in the mind, and might as well be images or
statues. And any who do attend sit all the time merely hearing, and
when they depart they remember nothing that has been said, and
in fact their object in coming was to please their sense of hearing
rather than to gain any profit; thus their soul is unable to conceive
or bring to the birth, but the moment the cause which stirred up
pleasure is silent, their attention is extinguished too (Philo *Congr.*
13.64–66 [Colson and Whitaker, LCL]).

Speakers, however, are not always successful. In *Diodorus Siculus* 18.67,
Phocion attempts to silence the crowd, but the crowd is unable to hear the
words because of the noise. They can, nevertheless, see Phocion's gestures
as he made his defense.[18]

Speakers are taught to engage their attention to help them overcome
distractions (Aristotle *Rhet.* 3.14.9–10; *Rhet. Her.* 4.16.24) so as to ensure
that the people did not respond disapprovingly (Cicero *De Or.* 2.83.339).[19]

A dinner guest comes prepared to listen and interact with the host
like a person playing catch with a ball. He is a "fellow-worker" with the
speaker (Plutarch *Mor.* 1.45E).

Likewise, students are taught to come prepared to listen as more
than passive observers (Plutarch *Rect. rat. aud.* 3 *Mor.* 38E) to help prepare them to speak. Good listening leads to good rhetoric and eventually
moral formation as we will see when we discuss this topic.

The payoff, of course, is an attentive audience that anticipates the
speech until the last word (Aristotle *Rhetoric* 2.23.1400b30). Cicero
remarks:

The ears of the city, therefore, we found hungry for this varied type
of oratory, displayed equally in all styles, and we were the first,
however, poor we may have been and however little we may have
accomplished, to turn them to an amazing interest in this style of
oratory. (*Brutus Orator* 30.106 [Hubbell, LCL])

18. Cf. Euripides *Hecuba* 545.
19. Maxwell, *Hearing Between the Lines*, 62.

Respond

Applaud

The most popular form of response to a speech is applause. Audiences hold their applause until the delivery of epigrams or memorable sayings (Quint. *Inst.* 8.5.2, 3, 13–14; 5.13.42; Cicero *De or.* 2.83.340).[20] At the conclusion of a speech, the audiences acclaim speakers who lead them along, causing them to anticipate the conclusion without spoiling the end prematurely (Aristotle *Rhetoric* 2.23.1400b30).

Fill gaps

Sometimes the rhetorical figures the speaker use, noted above, leave gaps for their audience to fill. These include facts the audience understands but are not presented in the case (*Rhet. Her.* 1.9.14), a puzzle the listener is trying to solve (*Rhet. Her.* 4.54.67), or an enthymeme (*Rhet.* 1.1.11; Quint. *Inst.* 5.14.1–2).

The enthymeme is a rhetorical proposition with a rationale that has no formal conclusion (Theon *Progym* 99–100). To supply the logical conclusion directly in the speech insults the intelligence of the audience.[21] The effect creates a "cooperative effort between the speaker and the audience" to co-create the meaning in performance. Unless the audience supplies the missing conclusion, the speech falls on deaf ears.[22]

React

The third part of the response is reaction to the material. In some cases, the reaction is emotional sympathy (Ovid *Metam.* 9.325–392), awe, or delight at the wonderful story (Ovid *Metam.* 4.273).

Depending on their role with the speaker, the audience asks questions, corrects material, provides feedback, debates each other, or interrupts. For example, in *Daphnis and Chloe*, an old man shares a story, delighting the audience, who then responds by asking questions about the story (Longus *Daphnis and Chloe* 2.3–7). Apuleius describes a story rejected by one listener and accepted by another:

20. Shiner, *Proclaiming the Gospel*, 154–56. For a thorough discussion of applause lines and reactions in Mark see Whitney Shiner.

21. Witherington, *New Testament Rhetoric*, 165.

22. Maxwell, *Hearing Between the Lines*, 57.

> So ended Aristomenes' story. But his companion, who in stubborn disbelief had rejected his tale from the very start, remarked, 'that is the most fabulous fable, the most ridiculous lie that I have ever heard.' Then he turned to me: 'Now you are a cultured fellow, he said, 'as your clothes and manners show. Do you go along with that story?' "Well, I said, 'I consider nothing to be impossible…. But as for Aristomenes, not only do I believe him, by Hercules, but I am also extremely grateful to him for diverting us with a charming and delightful story…. I have ridden all the way to this city gate here, not on his back, but on my own ears.' (*Metam.* 1.20–21 [Hanson, LCL])

To further illustrate, Pliny invites friends to come to recitations that could last for three days (*Ep.* 3.18.4–5). During an exchange with Tacitus, Pliny revises and marks his speech and receives criticism and praise throughout the process (*Ep.* 7.20). Circulating his speeches among friends, he invites corrections (Pliny *Ep.* 9.10). Quintilian leaves pages blank anticipating corrections (Quint. *Inst.* 10.3.32). Therefore, feedback is part of the process of recitation, as noted by Pliny:

> The reader is made more keenly critical of his own work if he stands in some awe of his audience, and he has a kind of panel of experts to confirm his decision on any doubtful point. He receives suggestions from different members, and failing this, he can infer their various opinions from their expressions, glances, nods, applause, murmurs, and silence, signs which make clear the distinction between their critical judgment and polite assent (Pliny *Ep.* 3.5 [Melmoth, LCL])

When they like what they hear, the audience tells others and brings them to gatherings.

Remember

Just as the reader prepares his memory for delivery through a process of practice, repetition, recall, forgetfulness, and delivery, the audience remembers during the performance. They experience various degrees of memory much like the performer does.[23]

To move from the distracting ideas of the marketplace as noted above in Philo (*Congr.* 13.65), the audience moves from listening to memory. The process begins with note-taking and recall. In a conversation with

---

23. Bauckham, *Jesus and the Eyewitnesses*, 280.

Terpsion, Euclides takes notes, recognizes gaps in his recollection, and returns to Socrates. (*Theaetetus* 142d-143a). Recall merely fights against the disease of forgetfulness (Philo *Congr.* 8.39–40). Philosophers warn against the audience that comes only to jot notes or hear good ideas:

> Certain of them come to hear and not to learn, just as we are attracted to the theatre to satisfy the pleasures of the ear, whether by a speech, or by a song, or by a play. This class, as you will see, constitutes a large part of the listeners, who regard the philosopher's lecture-room merely as a sort of lounging-place for their leisure. They do not set about to lay aside any faults there, or to receive a rule of life, by which they may test their characters; they merely wish to enjoy to the full the delights of the ear. And yet some arrive even with notebooks, not to take down the matter, but only the words, that they may presently repeat them to others with as little profit to these as they themselves received when they heard them. ... But the true hearer is ravished and stirred by the beauty of the subject matter, not by the jingle of empty words (Seneca *Ep.* 108.6–7 [Gummere, LCL]).

Instead the audience is expected to correct stories from memory. They keep the ideas fresh in their imaginations. According to Ovid, the storyteller omits parts of a story; and the respondent amends the story and tells his own version from their memories (Ovid *Metam.* 12.539, 536–579). The outcome, much like for the orator, is to have a vivid imagination to be able to see people that one is remembering (Aristotle) or to bridge a gulf between past and present (Philostratus *Vit. soph.* 582).[24] They recall mental images, recreate in their minds the experience described by the performer, and move from listening to recall to memory.[25]

Aristotle notes,

> And those in love enjoy talking and writing and continually doing something concerned with the beloved; for in all such things they think, as it were, to have sense perception of the beloved. The starting point of love is the same to all; [it occurs] when [people] not only delight in the beloved's presence but delight in remembering one absent; and they are in love also when there is grief at absence (*Rhet.* 1.11.11.1370b [Kennedy]).

---

24. Webb, "Imagination and Emotions," in Braund and Gill, *Passions in Roman Thought*, 117.

25. Ibid., 118.

When a performer is reading, he is not simply delivering from his account of the facts. He also uses the audience's recall, corrections, and memory. Thus, the audience's memories are being affected as well as the performer's memory. Together they influence one another.

PAIDEIA IN PERFORMANCE

With performer and listener engaged in the process, what is the effect on each other? The purpose of a speech is not merely to attract a large crowd or to gain the audience's applause. Epictetus warns against both. A reader can be caught up in the applause and miss the performance's function for the speaker and the crowd:

> When you are in such a sorry state as this, then, gaping for men to praise you, and counting the number of your audience, is it your wish to do good to others? "Today I had a much larger audience." "Yes, indeed, there were great numbers." "Five hundred, I fancy." "Nonsense, make it a thousand." "Dio never had so large an audience." "How could you expect him to?" "Yes, and they are clever at catching the points." "Beauty, sir, can move even a stone." There are the words of a philosopher for you! That's the feeling of one who is on his way to do good to men! There you have a man who listened to reason, who has read the accounts of Socrates as coming from Socrates, not as though they were from Lysias, or Isocrates! "I have often wondered by what arguments ever—no, but by what argument ever—this form is smoother than the other!" You have been reading this literature just as you would music-hall songs, haven't you? Because, if you had read them in the right way, you would not have lingered on these points, but this is the sort of thing rather that would have caught your eye: "Anytus and Meletus can kill me, but they cannot hurt me"; and: "I have always been the kind of many to pay attention to none of my own affairs, but only to the argument which strikes me as best upon reflection." (Arrian *Epict. disc.* 3.23 [Oldfather, LCL])

With both parties' active, collaborative role, the performance shapes, educates, trains, and forms people in their culture. This process, called *paideia*, was used in the ancient world for culture, education, training, disciplining and suffering. With very little access to written texts, orators and readers shape each other through performances in schools, lectures, home, and the marketplace.

Paideia of the performer

Character formation

A trained orator is a model citizen and a good example for society. The speaker's *ethos* plays a significant role in persuasion; to be a good orator required being a "good man" (Quint. *Inst.* 12.1.1–3). Good character formation is developed through habitual practice, training and moral formation (Plutarch "How to Educate Children" 4 Mor. 2–3). The practice in the rhetorical and philosophical schools shapes orators as people to "learn to live as they learned to speak."[26]

Character, however, is more than good habits. Typically for trained orators, because they come from wealthy families and are part of the rhetorical schools, this kind of formation is limited to the freeborn. Society views those with good ancestry, wealth, and power as people of character. (Aristotle *Rhet.* 2.12–17; Dionysius, *Ant. Rom.*, 2.8–9). According to Cicero,

> For excellence in speaking cannot be made manifest unless the speaker fully comprehends the matter he speaks about. It follows that, if the famous natural philosopher Democritus spoke with elegance, as he is reported and appears to me to have spoken, those notable subjects of his discourse belonged to the natural philosopher, but his actually elegance of diction must be put down to the orator. (*De Or.* 1.11.48–49 [Sutton, LCL])

> Then at last must our Oratory be conducted out of this sheltered training-ground at home, right into action, into the dust and uproar, into the camp and the fighting-line of public debate; she must face putting everything to the proof and test the strength of her talent, and her secluded preparation must be brought forth into the daylight of reality. We must also read the poets, acquaint ourselves with histories, study and peruse the masters and authors in every excellent art, and by way of, practice praise, expound, emend, criticize, and confute them; we must argue every question on both sides, and bring out on every topic whatever points can be deemed plausible; besides this we must become learned in the common law and familiar with the statute, and must contemplate all the olden time, and investigate the ways of the senate, political

---

26. Hadot, *Ancient Philosophy*, 151.

philoisophy, the rights of allies, the treaties and conventions, and
the policy of empire. (Cicero *De Or.* 1.34.157–159 [Sutton, LCL])[27]

During the first century, Jewish people follow suit. The center of learning is a school-like system around meals in pockets of Judaisms. They do
not depend on regular pilgrimage to Jerusalem for festivals. Instead they
incorporate the Greek and Roman practices of small school settings in
homes and performances at meal settings much like the symposia. They
emphasize keeping Jewish laws and maintaining a Hebrew heritage, and
the methods are very similar to their Greek and Roman counterparts.
Josephus, who is educated near the Temple, is at the top of this class
of students (*Life* 8–12). Students around the region receive educations
blessed by the priests.[28] "Lovers of Learning are beloved by God, for they
have educated their minds toward what is excellent." (*Let. Arist.* 287).[29]
"Thus the ideal of *paideia* was practiced in order to educate the young and
shape them into being virtuous persons who would live according to the
ways of the fathers."[30]

Divine contact

In addition to forming a person with good *ethos,* a good memory gives a
person access to the divine. As Frances Yates writes, in the ancient world
the soul had a remarkable power to remember things; and this was proof
of its divinity.[31] Memory is a divine power given by gods to the humans
along with energy, wisdom, and discovery.[32] Performances "spring to
birth" what is already inside the person (Cicero *De Or.* 2.87.356). Thus
the quest for wisdom leads to *paideia,* instruction, immortality, contact
with God, and a kingdom. (Wis. 6.17–20; Philo *Contempl.* 3.25). Feeling,
intelligence, life and energy are also considered divine. (Cicero *Tusc.*
1.27.66; Plutarch *Is. Os. 77 Moralia* 382D). In fact, memory allows people
to think about God even while they are sleeping (Philo *Contempl.* 3.27).

27. For other examples of *paideia* and character formation see Aulus Gellius *Noct.
att.,* 1.9.8; 1.26, 1–111; Arrian *Epict. diss.* 1.10,8; 1.26.13; 3.21–22; Porphyry *Vit. Plot.* 14,
10 , 3, 35; Plato *Tim.* 24c; Plutarch *Is. Os.* 382d.

28. Carr, *Origins of Scripture and Literature,* 284.

29. Dibelius and Conzelmann, *The Pastoral Epistles,* 143. Alexandre, "Rhetorical
Argumentation in Philo," in Caquot, Hadas-Lebel, and Riaud, *Hellenica et Judaica,* 27.

30. Flavius Josephus, *Life* 8–12 (Mason, Flavius Josephus), 271–272.

31. Yates, *Memory,* 45.

32. Ibid. Small, *Wax Tablets,* 133.

The soul lacks only the power to see itself. But like the eye, the mind, while not seeing itself, perceives other things. It cannot see, what matters least, its own form, though perhaps it can see that too, but let's not pursue the point- it certainly does see its power, acuteness, memory, motion, swiftness. These qualities are important, divine, everlasting. (Marcus Tullius Cicero, *Tusc.* 1.27.67 [Douglas])

For the Jewish audience, memory becomes part of renewal and obedience rituals. (Baruch 2.32 LXX). To remember, they recite divine names and meditate on acts of goodness, judgments, mercy, and kindness. (Philo *Spec. Leg.* 2.171; *Dec.* 62; *Sac.* 55,56).

Explanation of suffering.

Performances help explain how suffering is a part of the process of *paideia*. Children expect suffering to be part of their educational formation. Even memory, rhetoric, training, and disciplinary methods are interwoven at home as part of this formation. Fathers use suffering to discipline their children, train their memories, and control their anger and speech (Plutarch *[Lib. ed.]* 12–16; Moralia 9). Epictetus describes the experience like a surgery:

Men, the lecture-room of the philosopher is a hospital; you ought not to walk out of it in pleasure, but pain. For you are not well when you come; one man has a dislocated shoulder, another an abscess, another a fistula, another a headache. And then am I to sit down and recite to you dainty little notions and clever little mottoes, so that you will go out with words of praise on your lips, one man carrying away his shoulder just as it was when he came in, another his head in the same state, another his fistula, another his abscess? And so is it for this that young men are to travel from home, and leave their parents, their friends, their relatives, and their bit of property, merely to cry "Bravo!" as you recite your clever little mottoes? (Arrian *Epict. diss.* 3.23.31–32 [Oldfather, LCL])

Disciplining and whipping a son cause growth in character (4 Macc. 30.1); thus, the resulting suffering is viewed as the parent's compassion, discipline and shepherding (4 Macc. 18.13).

Paideia of the audience

Just as the performer is shaped in preparation for and during the performances, so are audiences.

Communities of readers

In the ancient world, some groups of elite audiences are invited to be a part of a literary club or circle called the *amici*. These groups form around people like Quintilian (*Inst.* 1.11–14) and his student Pliny (*Ep.* 1.9) to be involved in the editing and reading process. Being able to read and perform affords the performer and the listener certain privileges. As William Johnson notes, the reader proposes a topic, much like a book proposal. The audience adjudicates its value. The reader holds a writing event in a home during a dinner party or in an auditorium (Spurinna 3.1.9; Pliny *Ep.* 9.36.4; 9.40.2). Those who attend demonstrate their allegiance to the group leader or reader and validate the reader's status (Pliny *Ep.* 1.3.4; 2.10.4; 5.5; 5.8.7). The experience provides the elite person glory and recognition.[33]

In Jewish circles, however, the experience does not provide admission into a readers' club but an identity of suffering together and growth in brotherly love because of *paideia*. According to 4 Maccabees, "Since they had been educated by the same law and trained in the same virtues and brought up in right living, they loved one another all the more" (4 Macc. 13.22–26 LXX). They performed the scriptures and created a love of learning (Sir. 24.30; 30.1 LXX).

Emotional submission

By correctly using imagery and rhetorical figures, the speaker can take the audience to a beautiful place that transcends their current circumstances. The speaker can "enslave the audience" with his delivery.[34] Longinus writes,

> Now what is rhetorical imagery able to accomplish? It is equally able to bring into our speeches and writings what is characteristic of the courtroom and what is emotional, and when joined with attempts at practical arguments, it not only persuades the audience, it also enslaves it. (Longinus *[Subl.]* 1.4 [Arieti and Crossett)

---

33. Johnson, *Readers and Reading Culture*, 55–56.
34. Longinus, *[Subl.]*. 1.4 (Arieti and Crossett, Texts and Studies in Religion), 95.

Like Longinus, Quintilian teaches students to achieve "mastery over" their audience's imagery. The vivid pictures place the ideas before their minds where they "seem to show what happened rather than to tell it; and this gives rise to the same emotions as if we were present at the event itself" (*Inst.* 6.2.29–32; Similarly Quintilian *Inst.* 8.3.62,67; Aristotle *Rhet.* 3.11.1411b.20).[35]

Identification with a moral figure

By gathering in reading circles or philosophical groups, audiences in the ancient world identify and validate people as moral examples to follow. In the case of Pliny and the *amici*, the audience's attendance gave recognition and honor to the one assembling the group (noted above: Pliny *Ep.* 9.36.4; 9.40.2).

The moral example functions like a father setting a virtuous model for his children (Plutarch *Lib. educ.* 20). They look at the person much like a person gazes into a mirror. The reader helps the listener examine his life, reflect on his condition, remember what he looked like before he gazed into the mirror, and then change (Plutarch *Rect. rat. aud.* 5 *Mor.* 38E; Seneca *Ep.* 3.2.35.6–3.2.35.4).

In religious settings, such as the *Theraputae*, the person explains the meaning of laws that penetrate into the listener's soul. People respond with nodding heads and an "eager look in their eyes." They respond by identifying with the group and abiding by its rules (Philo *Contempl.* 3.25).

In philosophical circles, obviously the philosopher becomes an example that people follow and emulate. He draws them to himself by reputation through his effect on the listener. According to Epictetus,

> Does a philosopher invite people to a lecture? Is it not rather the case that, as the sun draws its own sustenance to itself, so he also draws to himself those to whom he is to do good? What physician ever invites a patient to come and be healed by him? Although I am told these days the physicians in Rome *do* advertise; however, in my time they were called in by their patients. "I invite you to come and hear that you are in a bad way, and that you are concerned with anything rather than what you should be concerned with, and that you are ignorant of the good and the evil, and are wretched and miserable." That's a fine invitation! And yet if the

---

35. For the connection between emotion and moral character in Aristotle, see Grimaldi, *Aristotle Commentary*, 12–13.

philosopher's discourse does not produce this effect, it is lifeless and so is the speaker himself. Rufus was used to say: "If you have nothing better to do than to praise me, then I am speaking to no purpose." Wherefore he spoke in such a way that each of us as we sat there fancied someone had gone to Rufus and told him of our faults; so effective was his grasp of what men actually do, so vividly did he set before each man's eyes his particular weaknesses . . . Men, the lecture-room of the philosopher is a hospital; you ought not to walk out of it in pleasure but in pain . . . Well! But isn't there such a thing as the right style for exhortation?—Why yes, who denies that? Just as there is the style for refutation, and the style for instruction. Who, then, has ever mentioned a fourth style along with these, the style of display? Why, what *is* the style for exhortation? The ability to show to the individual, as well as to the crowd, the warring inconsistency in which they are floundering about, and how they are paying attention to anything rather than what they truly want. For they want the things that conduce to happiness, but they are looking for them in the wrong place. To achieve that must a thousand benches be placed, and the prospective audience be invited, and you put on a fancy cloak, or dainty mantle, and mount the speaker's stand, and paint a word-picture of—how Achilles died? By the gods, I beseech you, have done with discrediting, as far as it is in your power to discredit, words and actions that are noble! There is nothing more effective in the style for exhortation than when the speaker makes clear to his audience that he has need of them. Or tell me, who that ever heard you reading a lecture or conducting a discourse felt greatly disturbed about himself, or going out said, "The philosopher brought it home to me in fine style; I must not act like this any longer"? But does he say to a companion, if you make an unusually fine impression, "That was beautiful diction in the passage about Xerxes"; and doesn't the other answer, "No, I preferred the one about the battle of Thermopylae"? Is this what listening to a philosopher amounts to? (Arrian, *Epict. diss.*, 3.23.27–38 [Oldfather, LCL])

As groups form, they create group identities and a collective social memory through ritual, stories, and monuments. These "sites of memories" become important activities, performances, and objects as the communities shaped their identities around a person or a group.[36] Like the architectural images and places in the heart of the orator, the groups' identities are shaped around a pattern that can be repeated in performance. In a

---

36. Mendels, *Memory*, 76–77.

recitation the audiences participate in collective acts of memory that explain what they are experiencing either as suffering or moral change. (Exodus 12.14–17; Deut 6–8 LXX). As they remember God, they become aware morally and have the capacity to change (Deut 4.33–40; 5.11–6.1 LXX).

Virtuous formation

These performances disarm the storyteller's opponents, move the listeners to educate the audience, or motivate the audience to act virtuously. For opponents who scoff and mock, a good story can disarm the listeners (Ovid *Metam.* 8.61–735).

In another example, when a gossip interrupts and questions the story teller, the gossip reveals her tricks to the one overhearing the interaction. "With my eyes uncovered, I could now freely observe all the tricks of that woman" (Apuleius *Metam.* 9.22 [Hanson, LCL]).

Hardships and sufferings because of bad choices or difficulties in life are viewed as a parental curriculum of *paideia*. The lessons learned from home and school carry over into life (Plutarch *[Lib. ed.]* 12–16 *Mor.* 9) Performances shape how they understand suffering and learning as *paideia*, shaping their identity.

Jewish groups explain suffering similarly as parental roles of discipline and education. They perceive discipline or suffering in the community as growth in character (Sir. 30.1–7; 4 Macc. 13.23 LXX). Even if the suffering results from sin, in 2 Maccabees the Lord can use it for educational (*paideia*) purposes (2 Macc 7.31–33 Prov. 19.18; 29.17 LXX).[37]

The performance's ultimate outcomes are change and moral decision-making. In performance, justice, self control, training in courage, piety, and reverence to God are taught (4 Macc. 5.22–30; 7.31–34 LXX). To gain the attention of the listener and begin to move them toward these changes, a speaker can use maxims. For example Seneca suggests the maxim, "He needs but little who desires but little" to change a person's love of money and greed. If an audience applauds or responds with wonder to the maxim, they are signaling greater interest and heightened awareness.

37. 2 Macc 6.12 views punishment as discipline. The Lord waits for other nations to punish them. He intervenes with discipline on these people as a parent. Also Prov. 1.2,7,8; 4.1 LXX; Prov. 16.17; 13.24, 3.11–12 LXX; Wisdom of Solomon is concerned for instruction in love that keeps laws and immortality connected with Wisdom (Wis 6.17–19).

Seneca encourages the speaker to use more rhetorical figures at this point and more examples to "strike home" until the orator has progressed and won over the audience to the honorable and upright (Seneca *Ep.* 108).

A good example of this occurs in the second century account of Aristides' appeal to Marcus Aurelius on behalf of the Smyrnans. Aristedes uses powerful visual imagery to make his case. He invites the emperor to use his memory to "summon mental images" from his visits to the city. This example is one of the few cases from the ancient world in which we have a record of both a speech and the performance provided by Philostratus.[38]

First, Aristides draws upon his memories and took him on an imaginary tour to motivate the emperor to rebuild Smyrna.

> Still even in these circumstances the god of fortune preserved one thing for it, almost like a token of salvation. You saw the city. You know the loss. Remember what you said when you viewed it on approaching, remember what you said when entered, how you were affected, what you did. (Aristides, *Works*, 19.2–3 [Behr])

He then takes him on a geographical tour of the harbor, the streets, the marketplaces, the gymnasiums and other sites that are destroyed. Interestingly the architecture of the city, an important mnemonic device in Quintilian is used by Aristides to help the emperor visualize the surroundings.[39]

According to Philostratus, the emperor is moved to tears upon reading the letter when he uses visualization (*ekphrasis*) through memory with the phrase, "She is a desert through which the west winds blow" (19.3) (Philostratus *Vit. soph.* 582 [Wright, LCL]).[40]

The *ekphrasis* has an effect on the listener. Webb states,

> The gulf between past experience and present circumstance is momentarily bridged in the mind of the recipient. An absent sight is recalled in order to inspire the audience to recreate the original experience from which the image derived, in this case by revisiting

---

38. Webb, "Imagination and Emotions," in Braund and Gill, *Passions in Roman Thought*, 116.

39. Aristides, *Works*, 10–11.

40. Ibid.

or recreating the city. The realization of the gulf between past and present is intended to arouse emotion and so inspire action.[41]

In the example above, the visual, emotional, and mental come together. By seeing the picture of the city, the emperor takes action to rebuild Smyrna.

THE SIGNIFICANCE AND LIMITATIONS OF ANCIENT PERFORMERS AND AUDIENCES

For ancient Mediterranean audiences, performances provided an opportunity to shape their cultures. Whether Greco-Roman or Jewish, people came armed with hungry ears; attentive faces; and most importantly, a good memory to listen, correct, applaud, and respond. Their memories were gifts of the gods, and they used them as part of the collaborative process. So much of the performance depended on the lector's adaptation of the conventions of rhetoric to the audience and the audience's response to the reading. If an audience was not listening, the performance was in vain. If the performer could effectively use emotions and impersonations, the audience could listen effectively.

Effective delivery and memory were the rewards of ancient rhetoric. When reader, audience, and performance came together, something happened. Stories were told, memories were shaped and formed, and individuals changed. Readers adapted their speeches to the audience, and the audience reshaped their memories around the performance and in many cases the figure. They gazed into the mirror of the performer and made decisions accordingly. The audience brought something to the room as well. Their listening skills, responses, memories, and reactions shaped and formed each other. What we might call a collaborative process today was more than a pooling of ideas or simply a performance and reaction event. Both were shaped together and found a common identity the more they interacted.

What were the signs of a good performance? We could pose a different question: do the texts give the audiences and the performers helpful handles to guide a good performance? From our reading of the ancient world, gestures, emotions, figures, and *testimonia* play a critical role in shaping the audience. From the audience's perspective, the

41. Webb, "Imagination and Emotions," in Braund and Gill, *Passions in Roman Thought*, 117.

gaze, the responses where noted, and their memories indicate strong receptivity to the message. Even where there is confusion or antagonism, the audience is at least engaged. The worst things that could happen in performance were apathy or distraction. The process involved the components of good communication and good listening, but both audience and performer expected each other to come to the performance to do their part.

Orators in the ancient world, however, were limited to the best, wealthiest, and brightest men. The schools of the *amici* and most Hellenistic Jewish groups were male clubs. Even with the gift of the gods, the listener was on his own to respond and reshape who he was. Without a good performer, a virtuous moral example, a philosophical school, or a rhetorical school, the listener was left, as Philo expressed, to be distracted by a world of ideas. Fathers in the ancient world disciplined for their benefit and to teach male children laws and statutes from their history. Very little development guided people beyond ethnic boundaries. Early Christian audiences knew of the perils and practices of performance in the ancient world but reshaped their performance around the activities of Jesus and saw the performance as his part of the work of memory.

3

Delivery and Memory in Early Christian Performances

"Looking to Jesus the pioneer and perfecter of our faith."

Hebrews 12.2

AS WE HAVE SEEN from our overview of the ancient world, performances drew upon the collective memories of people, involved reaction from the audience, and formed and shaped the orator before and during the performance. Like the audiences in the Greco-Roman world, the early Christian audiences responded and retold the stories; and they remembered others' stories and corrected each other. Early Christian texts reflect these conventions, but the performances in early Christian communities affected them in different ways than might be expected of someone educated in Roman culture or Hellenistic Judaism. Early Christians gathered primarily at tables, and the performances reframed their memories. Audiences retold, paraphrased, and responded to the message. The performance linked people in a chain of virtuous lives as part of an emerging community. They learned that hardships were more than difficulties or punishments. They were part of the curriculum of early Christian *paideia*. The performance fixed their attention on Jesus as a parental figure, teaching them and disciplining them in performance, and connecting them to one another and to him. The early Christians in turn formed communities around this central figure. For Greco-Roman or Jewish performances, the lector and audience shaped *paideia* around

39

their values. For early Christians, the performances shaped *paideia* around Jesus.

AN EARLY CHRISTIAN PERFORMER'S DELIVERY

For characteristics and examples of early Christian performance, we look to several texts that reflect these conventions in the ancient world. The performers gesture, recite, and remember as an audience expects in the ancient world. Early Christian communities listen, respond, and remember these works as part of the performance.

Consider several examples from early Christian writings. The Antioch church follows the practice of reading a letter aloud (Acts 15.31). Paul commands the recipient of the Thessalonian letter "that this letter be read to all of them" (1 Thess 5.27). Colossians is not only a circular letter for distribution but also a performance: "When this letter has been read about you, have it read also in the church of the Laodiceans; and see that you read also the letter from Laodicea." (Col 4.16). Luke depicts Jesus reading in the synagogue like a lector with an unrolled scroll (Luke 4.17–20). Timothy is urged to devote himself to reading scripture publicly (1 Tim 4.13–16).

The early Christian lectors perform for audiences at meals (Acts 2; Acts 4; Rom 15; 1 Cor. 10.21) in a manner that echoes the symposium tradition in Mediterranean cultures. The meal is served, and the entertainment or instructions follow.[1] The importance as we will see below is not the location of the recitation but the function of the reader's use of the body, rhetorical figures, and memory in performance. We will show how early Christian literature uses these same conventions from ancient reading to shape early Christian communities. In early Christian settings, a performer used his body, rhetorical figures, and memory much like the ancient world's communicators.

---

1. Johnson, *Religious Experience*, 168.

Gestures.

The book of Acts mentions several implied and explicit gestures that a lector performed as part of the conventions of recitation. Six times Acts specifically cites the gesture "he extended the hand to them." Each occurs prior to a deliberative or a judicial speech, and there are varying responses to each gesture (12.17; 13.16; 19.33; 21.40; 24.10; 26.1).[2] In performance, several implied gestures are used. Stephen kneels in Acts 7.60 as a sign of surrender. Paul shakes his cloak after opponents revile him (18.6), much like the priests did in Lysias (*Against Andocides* 51–53). A town crier quiets the crowd in Ephesus (Acts 19.35), implying a gesture for silence, likely an upraised fist with the fifth finger pointing upward (Plutarch *Mor.* 207e; 3 Macc. 6.1; *Wars* 2.611). Paul says farewell to Ephesus in Acts 20 with gestures of clasped hands and kneeling (Euripides *Hipp.*322–360; Sophocles *Oed. Tyr.* 758–765).

Face.

In Acts, Paul sizes up the council in a defense speech with a gaze to anticipate how the accusers are going to treat him (Acts 23.1), much like the sophist Fronto explained. This tactic was used when deciding how to make a defense (*ad M. Caes.* 3.6 [Haines, LCL]).

The phrase "from the mouth" or "by the lips" often functions as an organ of speech in early Christian literature (Luke 1.64, 70; 4.22; 11.54; *1 Clem.* 18.15; Matt. 5.2; 12.34; 13.35; 15.11b; Acts 8.35; 10.34; 18.14. Rom 10.8; Eph 4.29).[3]

Voice.

In Galatians, Paul wishes to be present in the room to deliver his speech so that he can "change his tone." Paul cries out to the audience during a defense speech in Acts (23.6). James refers to wages crying out against the rich (James 4.6). The barren woman shouts and cries for joy (Gal. 4.27). People cry out to God in the spirit of adoption (Rom. 8.15). The angel shouts a lament over fallen Babylon in Revelation (18.2), and the multitude shouts praise after Babylon's fall (19.1).

---

2. See my work on gestures, *Reading Acts,* 139–54.

3. BADG, s.v., "στόμα," 769.

Rhetorical Figures

Sorites.

As speakers perform these texts, they imitate several rhetorical figures. The *sorites*, or the chain-link effect, connects virtues and vices to show how one builds on the other.[4] In Romans, Paul uses *sorites* to summarize the virtuous life (5.3–5; 10.14–15; 8.29–30).

In an allegory that uses the *sorites* figure, the Shepherd of Hermas contrasts a chain of virtues to the chain of vices. In an allegory in *Vis.* 3.8.6, an ancient lady explains a vision of seven women called the daughters of Faith who support a tower representing the church. In this case, the *sorites* functions as the trope to explain a building metaphor:

> Their powers are supported one by the other, and they follow one another according to their birth. From Faith is born Continence, from Continence Simplicity, from Simplicity Innocence, from Innocence Reverence, from Reverence Knowledge, from Knowledge Love (*Vis.* 3.8.7 [Lake, LCL]).

The chain of virtues builds much like a *sorites* to the climax of love. In this context, much like the others, a Christian catalogue is spoken to a listener beginning with faith and ending with love.[5]

> "Listen," said he, "to the names of the stronger maidens who stand at the corners. The first is Faith, the second is Temperance, the third is Power, the fourth is Long-suffering, and the others who stand between them have these names: Simplicity, Guilelessness, Holiness, Joyfulness, Truth, Understanding, Concord, Love. He who bears these names and the name of the Son of God, shall be able to enter into the Kingdom of God." "Hear, also," said he, "the names of the women who have black raiment. Of these also four are more powerful. The first is Unbelief, the second Impurity, the third Disobedience, and the fourth Deceit; and those who follow them are called Grief, Wickedness, Licentiousness, Bitterness, Lying, Foolishness, Evil-speaking, Hate" (*Sim.* 9.15.1–3 [Lake, LCL]).

---

4. See Witherington III, *New Testament Rhetoric*, 230–31.

5. Bauckham, *Jude, 2 Peter*, 176.

In Clement of Alexandria, the *sorites* functions as a way to demonstrate the chain-link effect of character formation through wisdom. He draws on memory from *testimonia*[6]:

> But knowledge conveyed from communication through the grace of God as a deposit, is entrusted to those who show themselves worthy of it; and from the worth of love beams forth from light to light. For it is said, "To him that hath shall be given:" (Luke 19.26) to faith, knowledge; and to knowledge, love; and to love, the inheritance. (*Strom.* 7.10.55)

The *sorites* can also be used to explain vices to the Shepherd and help him understand how these "spirits" take up residence where the Holy Spirit can dwell:

> Hear then . . . Ill temper is first foolish, frivolous, and silly; then from silliness comes bitterness, from bitterness wrath, from wrath rage, and from rage fury then fury being compounded of such great evils, becomes great and inexpiable sin. (*Man.* 5.2.4 [Lake, LCL)

The list of vices in Romans can be performed as a *sorites* (Romans 1.19–20).

Allegories and Riddles.

Independent riddles are rare in the New Testament. When they occur, they are part of a larger argument within apocalypses or parables. For instance, the Jewish apocalypse 4 Ezra uses the familiar allegory of the soils (4 Ezra 9.16–18). Jesus uses a similar allegory of the soils to explain a parable about a sower and seed (Matthew 13/Mark 4/Luke 8). In each context, Jesus speaks enigmatically, prefacing the parable with the phrase, "Whoever has ears to hear," or "What do you think?" According to Tom Thatcher, these questions mark "riddling sessions" in the Synoptics and the Gospel of Thomas.[7]

---

6. Bauckham, *Jude, 2 Peter*, 175. Herm. *Mand.* 5.2.40 (chain of vices); *Vis.* 3.8.7. (chain of virtues). These lists encapsulate the ideal of a good life and the eschatological goal to the way of life. The Christian virtue of love is the climax. The Christian sorites begins with faith and ends with love. Herm. *Sim.* 9:15:2 Clem. Alex. *Strom.* 5.14.96; 7.10.55.

7. Thatcher, *Jesus the Riddler*, 32. Thatcher draws his conclusions based on the folklore traditions in oral culture. When read through the lens of rhetoric and performance criticism, Jesus' enigmatic questions are not always riddles. We will return to this in our analysis of Mark 4.

In Revelation, the listener writes a vision of the seven churches that he has seen and heard through allegories (Rev 1.12–20). Shepherd of Hermas (*Sim.* 5.2.1—5.7.3) hears parables that are difficult, and the listener asks repeatedly for explanations (5.3.1; 5.5.1). The answers are given allegorically.[8] We could also place in this category the allegory of Hagar and Sarah that Paul uses in Galatians 4.21–5.1 for its mystery and complexity.

Not all parables are allegories, of course; but the only parables in the New Testament are in the Synoptic Gospels, which will be discussed in the next chapter.

Visualization.

Early Christian writings include examples of visualization or *ekphrasis*. In Galatians, Paul publicly portrays Jesus as crucified (3:1). Hebrews visualizes the stadium or athletic arena (Hebrews 12.1–3). Revelation has seven visions, each one adding to and improving on the other one.

Characterization.

Impersonation is used in the New Testament for various purposes. In Romans 7, Paul impersonates Adam in his discussion of sin and the law (7.7–13).[9] In an exposition of Moses' sermon, the book of Hebrews personifies and impersonates the Holy Spirit (Heb 3.7–4.13).

The speeches in Acts are written as "speeches in character" or *prosōpopoiia*. Peter addresses the crowd following the sign of the Holy Spirit at the feast of Pentecost (Acts 2.14–40).[10] Two speeches occur in Acts 15, the account of the Jerusalem conference.[11] Peter offers a deliberative speech to the audience (15.7–11), and James responds to Paul and Barnabas (15.13–21). The reader in performance imitates James as he addresses the story audience in Palestine.[12]

---

8. Snodgrass, *Stories with Intent*, 53. Cf. *Vis.* 3.2.4–3.8.11.

9. Witherington III, *New Testament Rhetoric*, 132–133.

10. Witherington III, *Acts*, 138–139; Shiell, *Reading Acts*, 171.

11. Tannehill, *Narrative Unity*, 186.

12. Haenchen, *Acts*, 448; Tannehill, *Narrative Unity*, 192–193.

Memory

As in the Roman and Hellenistic Jewish world, the heart is the organ of memory (Luke 2.19; 2.51; Herm. *Vis.* 1.2.2; 3.7.6; Herm. *Man.* 4.2.2.; 6.2.8; Matt. 9.4; Testament of Levi 6.2; BAGD 403). Eusebius writes famously that Ireneaus made notes from Polycarp of Jesus' tradition "not on paper but in my heart" (Eusebius, *Hist. eccl.* 5.20.7)

The literature reflects a variety of ways to describe the memory process much like the ancient world: listen, recall, forget, practice, paraphrase, and remember. In Heb 10.32, the writer challenges the listener to recall previous good efforts as a way of motivating and inspiring the audience.[13] In 2 Peter 1:12–15, memory is used as a way to arouse the listener once the speaker has departed. The recipient knows the information but needs a reminder. In 2 Tim 2:8–13, Timothy's memory of Jesus Christ is based on the *testimonia*: "If we have died with him, we shall also live with him . . ." He is urged to "remind them of this" as a "worker." Clement of Alexandria refers to a "true tradition preserved in memory"[14] (Eusebius, *Hist. eccl.* 3.23.5).

In summary, the performance features in the ancient world are also present in early Christian literature's use of the body, rhetorical figures, and memory. Two features are distinctive. These performances largely took place around meals or in remembrance of Jesus' meal with his disciples. Visually and imaginatively, the table functions prominently. The figure of Jesus plays significantly in performance. In performance, the lectors impersonate Christian figures in performance and remember Jesus' words as *testimonia* along with words from Hebrew scripture.

ROLES OF THE EARLY CHRISTIAN AUDIENCE

The audience plays significant roles in early Christian performances. They listen, respond, interrupt, interact, remember, correct and provide feedback in performance. The community remembers the performance as a significant event as they develop.

---

13. Thompson, *Hebrews* 221.

14. Bockmuehl, "New Testament Memory," in Barton, Stuckenbruck, and Wold, *Memory in the Bible*, 346

Listen

The first goal of the speaker is to gain the listening ear of the audience (Acts 2.22; Matt 13.3/Mark 4.3; Acts 15.13; Acts 22.1; Acts 26.3; Rev. 2.2, 17, 29) or to regain their attention once it was lost (Gal. 5.1). An audience listens by watching the speaker (Luke 4), drawing near (Matt 5.1) or fixing their gaze or attention (Hebrews 12.1). In Revelation, the author pronounces a blessing on the reader and the listener (Rev. 1.3). Most of the time, silence requires a gesture (Acts 19.35; Plutarch *Mor.* 207e; 3 Macc. 6.1; *Wars* 2.611).

Listening is not always easy. In Acts 19.33, Demetrius the silversmith is unable to persuade the crowd that should do something about Paul and his companions. The crowd interrupts him much like any other crowd would do in the ancient world (Philo *Legat.* 243; Josephus *Wars* 2.402; 5.420; 7.42, 57).[15]

We can anticipate that like other audiences in the ancient world, listening was more than passive presence. They participate with varied responses.

Respond

Interrupt.

Most of the examples of responses presented here come from the speeches in Acts. In Acts 2, the crowd acclaims Peter by interrupting with a question: "What shall we do?" (2.37). We have already noted that the crowd responds to Demetrius with a stereotypical acclamation (19.28): "Great is Artemis of the Ephesians." Festus interrupts Paul's defense before Agrippa (26.24). Paul's account of the incident in Acts supplies another view of the audience. Here Paul and Cephas debate, correct, and confront much like any other ancient audience (Gal. 2.11–12).

Fill gaps.

Several speeches in Acts are incomplete.[16] Stephen's speech ends with Jesus standing as the judge, not finishing with needed information but a vision (7.56). In Paul's speech at Pisidian Antioch, the audience is left to

---

15. Johnson, *Acts*, 348; Haenchen, *Acts*, 573, n.5.

16. See Kathy Reiko Maxwell's fine analysis of the gaps in the speeches in Acts (*Hearing Between the Lines*, 160–65).

conclude that Jesus is God's Holy One (Acts 13.16–41). Apparently the audience is drawn into the process because they ask Paul to return and further discuss the topic. The performance audience must fill in the gap of Paul and Barnabas' speech in Acts 15 to the Jerusalem council (Acts 15.12–13). The assembly is attentive, but we are left to assume the words. In the Areopagus speech, Paul is not only interrupted (Acts 17.32) but cannot complete his proofs of the resurrection.

Correct.

During performance, the audience is expected to avoid godless chatter (2 Tim 2.16) and to correct each other (2 Tim 3.16; *1 Clem.* 35.5–8). They rebuke one another (1 Tim 5.20) and confront disagreements (Gal 2.11).[17]

Remember

As the performer reads, the early Christian audiences remember. We discovered in the previous chapter that memory is a useful tool in training an orator, in the formation of their character, and the process of delivery. Performers deliver from their memories and interact with their culture as well as the audience's memories.

We also discovered that the audience had a role to play in the retelling. In the storytelling tradition,[18] and letter writing tradition,[19] audiences offer feedback and correct the speaker. We know that performances are more than monologues. Depending on the performance, there are boos, cheers, hisses. As Whitney Shiner and I have said previously, applause lines are presumably built into the performance as natural breaks for the speaker, usually around the *chreia*.

We can expect, of course, that the early Christian audiences are quite similar to others in their culture and that these texts are performed very similarly to other oral/aural texts in the late-first and early-second centuries.

---

17. Luke 1:57–80, 3:23–38. The loosened tongue of Zechariah is a moment of rhetoric, inspiring awe and the sublime and changing the memories of the past with Zechariah and John and reshaping the future behavior of the listener. In Aristotle, statements moved and impressed the listener when the statements were antithetical, brief, balanced, and applicable to life (*Rhet.* 3.11.1412b.20).

18. Hearon, "Storytelling in the Ancient Mediterranean World," in Thatcher, *Jesus, the Voice, and the Text*, 104. Hearon notes the performer does not recite words from a fixed page, but the audience is involved in a creative process.

19. Pliny, *Ep.* 3.5; 7.20; Pliny, *Ep.* 9.10; Quint. *Inst.* 10.3.32.

The discussion of early Christian memory begins with Jesus' famous logion visualized around the table with disciples when Jesus says, "Do this in remembrance of me" (1 Cor 11:23; Luke 22:19–20). The early Christian gatherings around the table reenact the meals, especially the last supper, with the disciples.[20] In the ancient world, reminding and remembering are naturally appropriate for farewell discourses, especially 2 Timothy 2:8, 14 and Acts 20:31.[21] For instance, as Paul said farewell, he evokes the Ephesian elders' memories of his experiences with the phrase "as you know" (Acts 20.17). These traditions are passed orally by memory.

In Hebrews 10.32, recollection of previous good efforts during times of suffering motivates endurance and inspiration.[22] The enemy of the community is forgetfulness. In this case, failing to reflect on the past is tantamount to forgetfulness. The audience reflects on their previous actions and sees the direct connection between memory and illumination.[23] This time the endurance is possible because they see a new reality of Jesus' endurance as theirs.[24] The writer of Hebrews echoes a similar process of memory as Philo. The process in performance begins with remembering or recalling the good deeds of faithful figures from the past. This long list functions like a *sorites* linking the people together and the community to the people. The memory is selective. The list climaxes with a focus on Jesus. In light of this focus, Hebrews mentions the outcome (13.7) of the faith of these leaders, reminding them of those who in performance "spoke the word of God to you" (13) to complete the memory process.

Was this process representative of early Christian performances or just an anomaly? The trend certainly continues as early Christianity emerges. For example, Porphry notes about the third century Christian philosopher Plotinus:

> In the meetings of the school he used to have the commentaries
> read, perhaps of Severus, perhaps of Cronius or Numenius or Gaius
> or Atticus, and among the Peripatetics of Aspasius, Alexander,
> Adrastus, and others that were available. But he did not speak just

20. Bauckham, *Jesus and the Eyewitnesses*, 281. Here Bauckham argues for the reliability of the oral tradition as historical evidence. Historicity is of little concern to me but rather perform-ability is.

21. Ibid., 196.

22. Thompson, *Hebrews*, 221.

23. Lane, *Hebrews 9–13* 298.

24. Thompson, *Hebrews*, 225.

straight out of these books but took a distinctive personal line in his consideration, and brought the mind of Ammonius to bear on the investigations in hand. He quickly absorbed what was read, and would give the sense of some profound subject of study in a few words and pass on. When Longinus's work *On Principles* and his *Love of Antiquity* were read to him, he said, "Longinus is a scholar, but certainly not a philosopher." When Origen once came to a meeting of the school he was filled with embarrassment and wanted to stop lecturing, and when Origen urged him to continue he said, "It damps one's enthusiasm for speaking when one sees that one's audience knows already what one is going to say"; and after talking for a little while he brought the sessions to an end. At Plato's feast I read a poem, "The Sacred Marriage"; and because much in it was expressed in the mysterious and veiled language of inspiration someone said, "Porphyry is mad." But Plotinus said, so as to be heard by all, "You have shown yourself at once poet, philosopher, and expounder of sacred mysteries." The rhetorician Diophanes read a defence of Alcibiades in Plato's "Banquet" in which he asserted that a pupil for the sake of advancing in the study of virtue should submit himself to carnal intercourse with his master if the master desired it. Plotinus repeatedly started up to leave the meeting, but restrained himself, and after the end of the lecture gave me, Porphyry, the task of writing a refutation. Diophanes refused to lend me a manuscript, and I depended in writing my refutation on my memory of his arguments. When I read it before the same assembled hearers I pleased Plotinus so much that he kept on quoting during the meeting, "So strike and be a light to men." (Porphry *Vit. Plot.* 14–15 [Armstrong, LCL]).

Another text that illustrates the roles of performer and audience is the early second-century document, 2 Peter 1.5–20. The writer gives a farewell address and final instructions before his departure. As the book is read to the community, the performer cites the visual (1.16) and the verbal (1.18) evidence from the "sacred mountain," presumably the Mount of Transfiguration, where those present hear the words "This is my beloved Son." The story audience and performance audience are not present to hear the voice, but the author links them to the experience in several ways and creates in performance a "site of memory."[25]

The text uses the rhetorical *sorites* to connect author and the audience to each other. He reminds them of the kinship that has developed

25. Bockmuehl, *Seeing the Word*, 183.

through their growth and conversion. As we have seen, *sorites* is a common device in Greco-Roman, Hellenistic Jewish, Qumran rhetoric, and early Christian rhetoric to link together the virtues of a person's life. One builds upon another (Rom 5.3–5; Jas 1.3–4; Gal. 5.22–23; Philo *Sacrif. Abel.* 27; Philo *Leg. Alleg.* 1.64; Wis. 8.7; 1QS 4.2–6; *1 Clem.* 62.2; Ep. Barn. 2.2–3).[26] In this case, however, before the list reaches a climax, the group is bound together in "brotherly love" (1.7). Much like 4 Maccabees 13.19–27, the group has a kinship that is usually reserved for bloodlines. They are bound together through the experience.[27]

Second, the performance visualizes the "sacred mountain" using an *ekphrasis* (2 Peter 1.17–18). The phrase functions like the architectural rendering of a room reserved for a person performing and remembering. The place of the mountain has been retained and has formed an impression on the mind of performer and listener (Quint. *Inst.* 11.2.10–34; *Rhet. Her.* 3.16–24). Just as the letter of Aristeas functions in a Jewish community in Egypt and the letter to the Emperor functions for Marcus Aurelius regarding the city of Smyrna, the letter of 2 Peter treats the event of the Transfiguration as a mnemonic site. The community visualizes an event as a part of their formation and identity as a community.[28]

He "arouses a memory," much like 2 Timothy, so that even after the writer is gone, the community may be able to "recall these things."[29] As they continually recall the voice, they are linked together and their lives are different. We see emerging the necessary connection between memory and conversion to following Jesus. Memory, as far as 2 Peter is concerned, involves recall and virtuous living. By performing the story of the transfiguration in this way, the reader is changing their patterns of conduct.

This memory is a selective memory, as one expects from performance. The memory that 2 Peter cites is not the content found in the Gospels. Each one of the Synoptics remembers the Mount of Transfiguration differently and reframes the episode in light of an ongoing biography of Jesus. The recollection in 2 Peter does not include the embarrassing/humorous in the

26. Witherington III, *1–2 Peter,* 307.

27. Davids, *2 Peter and Jude* 177, 178, 182

28. Mendels, *Memory,* 78. 2 Peter cites one critical event in the life of the disciples as the defining event for the early church.

29. Bockmuehl, "New Testament Memory," in Barton, Stuckenbruck, and Wold, *Memory in the Bible,* 357–58.

Gospels' account of the apostles wanting to remain on the mountain. The focus is on the virtuous *sorites* and the voice.

Just as the *sorites* binds them in brotherly love to each other and the list, the *ekphrasis* continues the theme. Together they are taken visually to the event on the Mount of Transfiguration.

Third, the performance overcomes forgetfulness. The story reflects the event's importance for the community. They view memory as the recollection of a voice as shaping their memories, arousing them by way of reminder, preparing them to receive an eternal welcome, and overcoming spiritual nearsightedness and forgetfulness. As we have seen in Philo, forgetfulness is just as much a concern as distraction. They need a way to arouse their memories and keep the issues in their lives. The episode's content does not concern the performance audience. Historically, it quite frankly did not matter. What does matter, however, for this writer is the memory of the voice. In this case, the intended effect seems to be mentioned in the text. The listeners are called to "add to" and increase in the classic virtue ethics dominating the discussion in Colossians, Romans, and Galatians. This case, however, involves another exegetical feature.

Neither author nor story audience is present at the Transfiguration. They are called to remember a voice that they have only heard about from others. The performance connects the audience with the memories of those who are present to see and listen.[30] What is so fascinating about this episode is not that the Transfiguration happened. We have accounts in the Gospels for that. What is fascinating and compelling for us is that the early Christians, the listeners of Peter's testament, are encouraged to view themselves as a link in the chain of unbroken testimony about the event. This story audience is not the Gospel performance audience. This is another audience entirely who has heard the events passed down in performance. As the writing is performed, there is a shape or function to the recollection very similar in the way that memory and retelling shape the Hellenistic Jewish and the Greco-Roman listeners. Just as the virtues are listed in a rhetorical chain link, so the listeners are linked together back in time to the Transfiguration and forward to the Parousia (and the intervening generations).[31] Those who hear the performance are linked through their collective memories. In 2 Peter's case, what matters is not

---

30. Bockmuehl. *Seeing the Word,* 169–170.

31. Bauckham, *2 Peter,* 216.

the voice's historical audition but the performed voice recited to the audience to resound in their ears. The collective retelling, remembering, and virtuous living make the sacred mountain a place and performance to remember.

In summary, listening, responding, and remembering are part of the early Christian performances. Much like the Greco-Roman and Jewish audiences, the early Christian audiences had a part to play. We have illustrated as they gather primarily around tables, remembering Jesus' gathering with disciples, they enact what he taught them to do much like other listeners. In early Christian communities, readers recite and paraphrase texts, remember the outcome of the lives of significant figures in Israelite history, and connect their lives to the story. They remember stories and sites from Jesus and the disciples that take on new meaning as they are performed. These incidents function as memorial sites and reenactments. The process overcomes the tendency to forget and preserves their memories as these events are repeated.

PAIDEIA IN PERFORMANCE

Performances for some communities in the ancient world carried greater significance. For informed audiences and trained readers in philosophical and religious circles, the process functioned as *paideia*. The same could be said of early Christian gatherings. We have seen that performer and listeners played their parts. As they did, something happened when the texts were read to the early Christians.

These performances were an integral part of early Christian *paideia*. In each one, a word is spoken and an audience listens, responds, and re-members. Eight passages in early Christian writing mention performance and *paideia* together: Eph 5.17–6.9; 1 Tim 4; Hebrews 10–13; Titus 2; 2 Tim 1–2; *1 Clem.* 35–56; Psalms of Solomon 3–16; and Shepherd of Hermas *Visions* 2. In these *paideia* passages, a text is read or performed using rhetorical figures, anticipating a response from the audience, and evoking memories of the writer, speaker, or listener. These passages give us a sense across a wide section of early Christian writings how the conventions of *paideia* for early Christian communities affected audiences in performance.

The reader's training rhetorically functions in an early community to qualify him as a lector for a Christian community and gives him the moral *ethos* and spiritual memories to influence the community. The community's *paideia* trains them to gaze on Jesus reflected in the performance to shape character, view some forms of suffering as divine parenting, connect memory to pious living, and link the community virtuously around Jesus.

Paideia of the Performer

According to Markus Bockmuehl, the leaders and lectors are the "guarantors of collective memory and tradition." As their events are performed from first-hand accounts, the "formative past [comes] alive and enable[s] the mutual validation of personal and collective memory."[32] Their memories are strengthened by the mandate that Jesus gave them and the continual commemoration of the martyrs' lives.[33]

We can see this in the *paideia* traditions associated with one of the prominent readers in early Christian writing, Timothy. He is presented as a lector being trained for the work of public reading of scripture (1 Tim 4.13–16). The scripture and the prophecy in this text are part of a rhetorical *testimonia* (Quintilian *Inst.* 5.11.37–44).[34] His training shapes his *ethos*. The speaker visualizes the gesture of "the laying on of hands" to convey its significance. The implied gesture is an act of memory. Timothy is trained to visualize and remember his training and empowerment ceremonially much like Moses' ritual of laying hands on Joshua in Numbers (27.18). In performance, the gesture connects the ritual from Numbers to a new teacher and community around Timothy.

Timothy is a new Joshua indeed, but also his audience is affected by recitation in this statement: "You will save both yourself and your hearers" (1 Tim. 4.16). By watching life and the progress of the teaching, the performance audience will be preserved. This point is clarified in an enthymeme:

Premise A: Pay attention to what saves you and your hearers.

---

32. Bockmuehl, "New Testament Memory," in Barton, Stuckenbruck, and Wold, *Memory in the Bible*, 352.

33. Ibid.

34. Witherington III, *Letters for Hellenized Christians*, 261.

Premise B: By paying attention to your life and teaching on an
ongoing basis, you save yourself and your hearer.

The audience fills in the gap or the conclusion: you ought to pay
attention to yourself and your teaching.

Because Timothy is so trained, his reading forms him and those listening.
The reading affects the one delivering. Teaching and way of life are the
tests of his faithfulness and the basis of his credibility.[35] Here his character
is reflected in the reading. As a reader, he becomes a mirror reflecting to
the audience how they should view their lives. His *ethos* is connected to
their reception. As Witheringon rightly notes the teacher's character matters and is connected with the reader's formation. The leader is formed,
and the listeners are affected.[36]

In another *paideia* passage in 2 Timothy 1:1–14, the writer dis-
cusses Timothy's *paideia* in light of memory, a relationship with Eunice
and Lois, and the writer's memory of Timothy. The writer reflects on his
relationship with Timothy and uses several words for memory. He "remembers" Timothy in his prayers, "recalls" his tears, is "reminded" of his
sincere faith, and wants to "remind Timothy." In this short passage, we get
the sense that memory is more than a way to begin a letter. As a listener
overhears the performance, the effect would be that he too is reminded of
something that he has heard before. Much like the passage from 2 Peter
1, when the audience is remembering what they have heard, Paul has
not given Timothy new information. Instead, much like a student in a
rhetorical school, he is delivering from his memory. Timothy has heard
something before through his grandmother Lois and his mother Eunice[37];
and the speaker draws upon previous experiences for a purpose. In this
case, remembering serves a purpose much like a campfire. By listening
and remembering, he "rekindles" or "fans into flame" a gift of God.

The language is reminiscent of the divine power of memory and recollection. In a world where audiences consider memory to be something
that one inscribes on a wax tablet on a heart (Prov 3:1–6) or on the soul
(Plato), Timothy's memory is not changed because of new information
but is rather a smoldering fire that is rekindled through the divine gift of
the spirit. In his relationship with Paul, at least in this text, his memory

35. Gloer, *1- & 2 Timothy-Titus 179.*

36. Witherington III, *Letters for Hellenized Christians,* 341.

37. Gloer, *1- & 2 Timothy-Titus,* 221.

does not need new information as if he needs to be shaped or changed. His memory is formed already and shaped through his relationship with his family who was presumably around even before Jesus. Indeed, Acts seems to suggest that this family was God-fearing Gentiles who observed Jewish law.[38] Instead of correcting that family or seeing some discontinuity between what they did and what Timothy is doing in Ephesus, the image of the campfire suggests that memory can be rekindled and can grow out of the smoldering fires of the past.

In this case, Timothy's relationship with Eunice and Lois becomes another site of memory for Timothy's formation and encouragement.[39] He and, by extension the listeners, are drawing on a spark (2 Tim. 1.6) that occurred in the family. This spark is ignited in the audience in performance. Timothy is viewed as a child in training rhetorically and spiritually. As the text is read and performed, the listeners too are taken back to their families or at least to their memory of Lois and Eunice to remind them of the spark of faith.

Paideia of the Audience

Four features of *paideia* shape the early Christian audience. They gaze on the lector and center their attention on Jesus shaping character. They are educated about their suffering as God's parental role. Their memory becomes an act of piety and moral change. They identify with a community that remembers together.

Character formation.

In Epictetus, Seneca, and Plutarch, the orator expects to hold the audience's attention, and the audience responded with a fixed gaze. Likewise the Christian communities respond with such attention (Luke 4) and were called to pay attention to Jesus as a moral figure[40] to help them endure difficulty[41] (Heb 12:2). Performance centers their attention on the work of Jesus (Heb 12.2). The idea of the gaze or "looking to Jesus" draws more than an attentive posture but also provides a moral figure around whom to identify their lives. Here Jesus functions in performance much

---

38. Gloer, *1- & 2 Timothy-Titus*, 221.

39. Mendels, *Memory*, 78.

40. Johnson, *Hebrews*, 345.

41. Thomson, *Hebrews*, 249.

like Plutarch describes those we are trying to emulate (Plutarch *Per.* 1–2). The example of Jesus and other faithful figures of the past functions as mirrors for these communities to reflect on their condition. The image of the mirror is popular in Christian circles (James 1.22–25) as a means of change. In this case, gazing on these examples allows the listener to recall behaviors and asses her condition.

This process fits the themes in a performance of Hebrews. Tasting the beautiful "word of God" rhetorically and the power of the coming age (1:32–35) gives them confidence and boldness during a time of deprivation as they remember those who spoke "the word of God" to them (13.7). In 12.4–12 they hear in performance (*paideia*) how to endure suffering. As they visualize Jesus' sacrifice and resurrection, the people become enlightened (Hebrews 6:4–5), taste a divine gift, and partake of the Holy Spirit.[42]

Fidelity to Jesus causes their attention to be on him and to discern right moral choices. The character of faith is understood as loyalty and endurance that perseveres through obedient faithfulness, not heroism. (3:1–4:13; 11:8–22). As opposed to someone like Esau, who loses patrimony over immediate gratification, (12:14–17) the character of faith demands "endurance as well as exclusive loyalty."[43]

Divine parenting.

In the ancient world, memory is a gift of God and part of a rational soul's divine nature. The individual progresses morally because of the divine attributes embedded in the person. In the Jewish communities (*Let. Arist.* 287; Prov 3.11–12 LXX; and Deut 8 LXX), people remember laws and statutes; and the father is the disciplinarian to enforce the rules. He enforces discipline because he loves them and desires for them to experience life as approved by God.

In early Christian circles, *paideia* in performance demonstrates that moral conversion is not only a gift from God but is impossible without ongoing assistance from God.[44] A person needs God's help to enable the virtuous life. In performance, the divine gift of God explains some forms of suffering as parenting.

---

42. Johnson, *Hebrews*, 166–67.

43. Johnson, *Hebrews*, 168

44. Ware, "Moral Progress in *Passions and Moral Progress* 278.

In the Psalms of Solomon, this link converges with Hebrew and Greek piety. Memory plays an important role in the Lord's discipline. The Lord "remembers with rebuking." (10.1–3). However, the Lord also protects as children are disciplined (*paideia*) in secret. Their memory is preserved, and life goes on forever (13.7). Remembrance of God involves continual prayer, repetition of events, and acceptance of suffering as educative. The process of remembering gives eschatological hope.[45] A similar effect is described in 1 Clement. In 1 Clement, Christ in the congregational prayer teaches (*paideia*) through a similar process: "You see, beloved, how great is the protection given to those that are chastened by the Master, for he is a good father and chastens us that we may obtain mercy through his holy chastisement" (56.16 [Lake, LCL]).[46]

Hebrews recognizes everyone, no matter what family of origin, is a true child of God. Everyone is also subject to the disciple from parent God. The discipline is for our benefit (Heb 12.10) as opposed to the secular father's discretion. Stress is placed not on human endeavor but in God's bestowing the gift of discipline to share in holiness. A person cannot share holiness without suffering. Correction through discipline is thus related to forming godly character.[47] Scripture is used to address people in their current conditions.[48] All forms of suffering are not educational. When people participate in Jesus' sufferings, they are being educated and formed along a path of discipleship (12.4–12).[49]

Growth in moral maturity involves a form of character transformation by learning through suffering (Heb 5.5–10).[50] Struggle against sin and maturity is like the discipline or education of sons in Greco-Roman *paideia*. The sufferings experienced in moral endeavors are analogous to a father disciplining the son he loves—with one exception. Echoing the same language for moral education used in 5.1–6.1, Hebrews regards suffering as a process by which the audience is being transformed into a 'sonship' like Jesus' (12.7). While it is going on, all instruction seems more a

45. Horbury, "Remembrance in Solomon," in Barton, Stuckenbruck, and Wold, *Memory in the Bible*, 121.

46. Dibelius and Conzelmann, *The Pastoral Epistles*, 143.

47. Lane, *Hebrews*, 421–423.

48. Thompson, *Hebrews*, 254.

49. Ibid., 256.

50. Johnson, *Hebrews*, 169

matter of grief than of joy. But for those who have been fully trained, it yields in the end the peaceful fruit that is righteousness (12.11).[51]

Memory and piety.

Early Christian writings suggest that the performance changes how memories are affected. In our study of Philo, we noticed how he uses the rhetorical device of allegory to remember figures differently. A character such as Joseph, Sarah, or Abram symbolizes an issue in a believer's life. As early Christian texts emerge, we see a pattern of reshaping memories of people and events. The memory of God and faithful Jewish figures become part of early Christian piety (*Pss. Sol.* 10.4, 16.6). Memory echoes the Septuagint and Psalms of Solomon combination of memory with piety. Memory is not merely recall of facts or prevention of forgetfulness. This is no longer a historical memory but a mystical one: "Although the historical judgment and mercies of God are not ignored, and in other psalms of Solomon the national dimensions of piety is strongly represented, the concentration in the passage quoted here from Pss. of Sol. 3, 6, 16 is on the present experience of the psalmist and the judgments and mercies known therein."[52]

Memory has implications for life. When someone remembers correctly, he is changing based on what he remembers. Memory brings the past into the present and is part of praise and commitment. Memory, praise and commitment come together as part of the performer and the listener's foundation of a virtuous life.[53]

Jesus' teachings and life become a part of this oral *testimonia*. Jesus' teachings are crafted so that "his hearers could take away, remember, ponder, and live by them."[54] Listeners recognize the sayings and apply these memories to practices within the community.[55]

The lives of those who exemplify his teachings and actions become "sites of memory" for the communities to emulate. As Quintilian, Aristides, and Cicero used the architectural layout of a city to describe and visualize the events of a place, the early Christian audiences view the

51. Talbert, *Learning through Suffering*, 72.
52. Horbury, "Remembrance in Solomon," in Barton, Stuckenbruck, and Wold 124.
53. Stettler, *Die Christologie* 170–71
54. Bauckham, *Jesus and the Eyewitnesses*, 202.
55. Ibid.

people-in-character (characterizations) and performances as living sites of memory. The outcome of their lives is visualized through the memories and stories told. As they were performed, they are brought to mind, and people viewed their lives as formational markers in the community's identity. Like the map of a city (Aristides "A Letter to the Emperors Concerning Smyrna" 19.2–3) used to remind an emperor of his responsibility toward Smyrna, the lives of exemplary figures function as a map to guide the behavior of early communities.

Hebrews is a good example. In performance, the audience hears examples of the outcome of the faithful people's lives (13.7). As they are addressed, the community emulates the behavior that results from their faith. The audience is not to imitate the ending of their lives, or every incident in their lives. Presumably, there are habits about each person that should not be imitated. Hebrews suggests a focus on the result of this way of life. No matter how each person lived his or her life, or whether a life ended in martyrdom, in performance the audience focuses on the result of their conduct.[56] In each life, the outcome is the same—faithful lives worth remembering and following. This outcome is the part of the curriculum of *paideia* for those listening to the "word of God" being spoken and performed to the community (13.7). Whether in lists of people as outcomes of faith, they also become the ways they remember who they are and how they are shaped. As they hear their lives performed and considering the implications, they are hearing "the word of God."[57]

Community identity.

As letters are read in the communities associated with Paul, Paul takes on the role of instructor with co-workers (Rom 16.3; 16.21; 1 Cor 3.9).[58] The effect is a binding together of love for one another as part of the revealed truth. Unlike philosophers who hold each other accountable, correct each other, and speak to one another, the followers of the Way place themselves in the midst of divine initiative that holds them together as texts are read. In 2 Timothy 3:16, scriptures from the Old Testament are suitable for Christian instruction, much like the mysteries were in the Greco-Roman world (Arrian *Epict. diss.* 3.12.15). The reader performing with them

56. Craddock, "Hebrews," 164.

57. Witherington III, *Letters for Jewish Christians,* 358.

58. Peerbolte, "Paul and Paideia in *Jesus, Paul, and Early Christianity,* 265.

readies them for service and equips them for good works. They correct each other out of mutual devotion to one another in light of God's grace (Titus 2.11; 2 Tim 2.25; Herm. *Vis.* 3.9.10). As Titus suggests, God's grace is the "driving force" in the early-Christian community's formation. The Greek ideal suggests self-actualization, satisfaction, and fulfillment, much like the self-help ideals of today. Instead, God's grace teaches, forms, and shapes the early communities' culture (Titus 2:11). Instead of a singular focus on knowledge of Torah as the primary source of information in some Jewish communities, the early Christians demonstrate that grace teaches, forms, and shapes lives.[59]

The community is not an elite *amici* circle but rather a group of readers bound by a common identity around the memory of Jesus. In a diatribe against heretics, Tertullian notes how quickly the catechumens moved from being a Deacon one day to a Reader the next (*Praescr.* 41). Eusebius cites readers in a list of other offices of the church (*Hist. eccl.* 6.43.11; Hippolytus *Trad. Ap.* 1.12).

Virtue lists link the community together rhetorically. They differentiate themselves from the larger world and rid themselves of greed and other vices. Using *testimonia* from an authoritative text, they teach each other who they are and establish an identity (Rom. 5.3–5; 1 Clement, 1 Timothy, Titus).

In Aristotle, praising a person for characteristics that the performer wants the person to have motivates action. In early-Christian circles, performers praise the gift that God has given them to allow faithful action. Performers displayed examples of people for others to follow because of a divine work that enabled emulation in community. The performance becomes part of the formation of the egalitarian community identified with Jesus where there is "neither Jew nor Greek slave nor free male nor female" (Gal 5.28). This community focuses on God-given memories and virtues to form and shape their lives.

Consider the use of *paideia* in performing two farewell speeches in Acts, Stephen in Jerusalem and Paul in Ephesus. In performance, Stephen functions as the trainer for his persecutor. Acts presents Stephen as a model orator who paraphrases the story of Israel and uses *testimonia*

---

59. Witherington III, *Letters for Hellenized Christians,*143. Cf. *Let. Aris.* 287 Josephus *J.W.* 7.343; Acts 7:22; Plato *Leg.* 741A Xeonphon *Mem.* 1.2.1. Note Plutarch *[Lib. ed.]* 12–16 on the punishments. Mott, "Greek Ethics and Conversion" 22–48.

from LXX to defend himself against the religious leadership.[60] Stephen has "words of wisdom"[61] that affect his interpretation of the Hebrew scriptures. As Jesus indicates in Luke, the Spirit will give "words of wisdom" in trying times (21.14–15). He paraphrases Israel's history as one would expect a trained orator to do, much like Theon had advised people to paraphrase and like Quintilian used *testimonia* that have the "conviction of truth" (Quint. *Inst.* 5.11.42). Their concept of memory or "recall" is a combination of paraphrase, dialogue, and debate. Several examples are seen in the early Christian performers' farewell addresses.[62]

Stephen uses *syncrisis* to compare his group of Jews to another Jewish group (Aristotle 1.9.38; Theon *Progymnasmata* 10).[63] Much like Plutarch (*Glor. Ath.* 1–8; *Mor.* 345c-351b) and Quintilian (*Inst.* 2.4.20–21) trained orators to compare various moral figures and characters side-by-side, the *syncrisis* helps the listener understand the difference between two ways of living.

Stephen casts himself along with Messianists who trace their lineage back to Abraham. They do not want to destroy the temple but rather renew the institutions. He stands in a long line of faithful Jews who now follow Jesus. On the other hand, the temple leaders are compared to Egyptians, Joseph's brothers, and grumbling Israelites. Although the Egyptians try to train Moses in Egyptian culture (*paideia*), a greater plan is at work. The experience trains Moses for leadership. Stephen stands in the line with Abraham and Moses. The opposition stands with those who have tried to go against God's will. Stephen does not deliver an anti-Judaic message but a comparative one among various groups within Judaism. Stephen is not trying to incite the crowd; he is carrying out what he is trained to do and what has become a response to other training.[64] Because *syncrisis* is taught in the rhetorical schools, the pattern is easily recognized by Saul who is about to be trained for a greater mission.

60. The defense speech has been well documented. Soards, Johnson, *Acts,* 140. Parsons, *Acts,* 89–108. Witherington III, *Acts,* 259–278.; Talbert, *Reading Acts,* 77–82.

61. Parsons, 87.

62. Bauckham, *Jude, 2 Peter,* 196. *Jub.* 22:16; 2 *Apoc. Bar.* 84:7–8; *Bib. Ant.* 19:5; 24:3; Josephus *Ant.* 4.318; John 14:16; Acts 20;31; 2 Tim. 2:8, 14; *Act. Verc.* 36. "The major concern of which that the speaker's teaching be remembered and observed after his death."

63. Parsons, *Acts,* 107–8. Witherington III, *Rhetorical Criticism,* 167.

64. Parsons, *Acts,* 107.

Just as Moses is trained for a greater purpose during the experience in Egypt and Saul is trained by Stephen's persecution, now Paul models Stephen's pattern in his farewell address to the Ephesian elders (20.17–38). Both speeches occur within the same narrative, contain examples of what an audience expects to see from a speaker, and give us insight into how a speaker's memory affects a performance and how an audience's memory would conversely affect a performance.

Rhetorically, the performance audience knows that the "words of wisdom" are associated an orator's trained memory. Stephen carries this out effectively through his recollection of Jewish history. How would Paul's memory be used in performance? Paul paraphrases a logion of Jesus and calls upon the elders' collective memories as he says farewell. He too paraphrases and draws upon their memories of him rather than Moses' memory. Their memories are a significant part of the argument. Paul draws on their memory of him: "You yourselves know" (20.17). He reminds them of the three years of admonition and work among them (20.31–34) and gestures with his hands when discussing his care for himself and others. Their memory becomes a part of the encomium's *peroratio* (conclusion), reminding them of a logion that does not appear in the canonical Gospels: "It is more blessed to give than receive" (20.35).

Fascinating connections occur between Stephen's and Paul's speeches in Acts. Both are farewell addresses; they draw on people's memories through *testimonia* and direct address to the audience; and they gesture to their audiences with a variety of emotions. Stephen kneels to speak to God, reminiscent of Jesus' kneeling address to the Father in Luke (22:41).[65] Paul kneels after he has reached out to the elders with a gesture and is kissed (20.36). In a fascinating and ironic turn, the kneeling Stephen is stoned in front of a consenting Saul. Now the kneeling Paul is kissed, blessed, and reconciled to elders in Ephesus. At the end of his speeches Paul, like Stephen, kneels, both using gestures of supplication. A lector performing the text does not perform as if Stephen begs for the people's mercy. He makes supplication on behalf of the people so that the Lord will show the people mercy. He kneels to the Lord, and the heavens open. Paul kneels in front of the Ephesian elders in supplication, and they greet him with tears.

---

65. Matthew and Mark depict Jesus on "his face" (Matthew) or "on the ground" (Mark).

Paul's speech contains not only the performance use of memory, but also the aspects of gesture and a parallel with Stephen's gesture associated with Saul/Paul.[66] The performance audience might have been prompted to connect Stephen to Paul when performed with similar gestures. The presentation in Acts suggests to a lector that the submissive Stephen is training Saul for future speeches at the hands of others.

Paul's link to the Stephen episode in Acts, however, can be brought into clearer focus in performance by the audience's *paideia*. Just as Moses is trained in Egyptian culture, so Stephen trains Saul in the pattern of the Way. Through a *prosōpopoiia*, the lector trains the listeners in new memories of Saul/Paul and a witness's conduct.

From the perspective of performance, the listeners are more than those in the story audience. As Stephen's face glows, he functions as the mirror to be held in front of Saul and the performer's audience, much like Plutarch, to reflect on their condition and to begin a process of change.

In performance, the reader has a variety of options to fulfill the audience's expectation. The *paideia* in performance comes as the lector presents a *prosōpopoiia* of Stephen's speech. This impersonation recreates the characters in the listeners' minds a "rhetoric of performance and presence."[67] In a performance of Acts, Stephen is linked geographically to the person attending his stoning, Saul. They both come from the region of Cilicia (Acts 6.9; 21.39). Saul is part of the audience and, from the perspective of Greco-Roman performance, is being trained as he watches a faithful figure die. Whether or not the historical Paul learned this way is immaterial. The link between the two suggests in the narrative that Saul's presence at Stephen's stoning not only places Saul/Paul at the scene of the crime but also provides Paul a model of Christian rhetorical training. The performance of both trains the audience.

The lector has several options, and the audience can respond in a variety of ways. Both speeches' emotions and rhetorical figures provide plenty of opportunity for amplification and illumination.

From the perspective of *paideia*, we can anticipate how the performance audience is trained. Stephen is an early example of how a speech affects an audience both positively and negatively. The speech trains those watching and affects those listening, and the performance also trains

---

66. Shiell, *Reading Acts,* 164–68.
67. Ward, "Pauline Voice," 101.

other people in the audience for future presentations. Jesus indicates that those facing trials will receive "words of wisdom" (Luke 12.11–12; 21.15). Stephen fulfills what Jesus said would happen, the accusers cannot withstand his "words of wisdom" (Acts 6.10).[68] In chapter 7, these words become *testimonia* from memory delivered in a defense speech. He paraphrases the listeners' memories of Joseph, Moses, and Israel. In Stephen's case, even though he may have anticipated a negative response, in the story above he demonstrates how to remain calm, focus on heaven, and submit to divine contact.

According to Acts 20, Paul carries out this training when he faces people who have bad memories of him (just as there were negative memories of Moses and Joseph). In this case, a different response can be expected. Paul receives a positive response. In performance, the audiences reframe their memories of Saul and others, like Moses and Joseph, who had terrible beginnings. As Hebrews indicates, the focus in performance is on the outcome of a person's life, not the way he dies or the specifics of a person's behaviors (13.7). So in performance, the audience learns how to remember the outcome of Saul/Paul's life as a result of the experience with Stephen and subsequent issues in Ephesus.

The audience learns how to recall, remember, and retell their traditions and their lives of faithfulness and challenge. If they face similar situations as Stephen and Paul, they use their memories to look to God for guidance and blessing in the process. They view suffering as parenting from God rather than punishment for sin or a sign of failure of the movement. They anticipate that some people will respond positively and others negatively. The lesson from Stephen and Paul can help them anticipate the responses in their world no matter the outcome.

Just as Stephen is an example of Jesus, is Paul now taking Stephen's mantle to meet persecution in Jerusalem at the hands of similar elders? Does Paul's life now come full circle with Stephen's? Does this story foreshadow a similar death of Paul? A reading in performance leaves the open-ended possibility for the audience to debate, discuss, and complete.

Much like Moses, their memory of Paul is changing. The performances reflect the same conventions of memory as Philo and Hebrews. Acts takes characters from the ancient world, paraphrases, characterizes, or shapes their memories, and affects how audiences view them

68. Talbert, *Reading Acts,* 76.

differently. No matter what they thought of Saul, they have another view of Paul. In performance, Stephen is the site of memory to reframe the old knowledge of Saul and the new identity of Paul. The Jerusalemites are opposed to Saul (9.26–27), but Barnabas informs a different view of Saul based on his ability to "preach boldly" and "dispute against the Hellenists" (9.28–29).

The Saul of Acts 7 is responsible for the death of one of the leading church deacons. The scandal, of course, is that Saul at some level could be accused of murder much like Moses was in Egypt. The Ephesian elders' blessing replaces the memory of Saul as murderer and bestows on Paul the mantel of blessing and affection. He is redeemed from his past; and he moves forward, ready to face the consequences of his decision to go to Jerusalem.

As a summary, the following chart lists eight texts with the *paideia* theme, each of which provides an example of *paideia*, performance, memory, rhetorical figures, and the effects on the story audience in early Christian communities.

Paideia and Performance in Early Christian Literature

	1 Tim 4:13–16	Heb 10–13	Eph 5.19–6.9	Titus 2:11–14	2 Tim 1:4–2:26	Pss. Sol. 3–16	1 Clem 35, 56	Herm. Vis. 2
Paideia	Teaching	Suffering	Children and fathers	Grace	Mother, grandmother	Lord, and the Listener, Righteous Discipline	God, sender	Lady Shepherd
Performance	Public Reading of scripture	Word of God	Psalms, Hymns	Teaching	Word of truth, Debates	Reciting the divine name, works of God	Spoken holy word	Reading a book
Memory	Gesture of hands, gift of God	Outcome of Jewish figures and leaders	*Testimonia* of Genesis, Exodus, Jesus	Coming of Jesus Christ, Epiphany	Campfire, *Testimonia*,	Pilgrimage, evening prayers	Remembrance before God, *testimonia*	Note taking, listening, recollection
Rhetorical figures	*Sorites*, Gesture	*Sorites*, *Ekphrasis*	Direct address, Household code	*Sorites*, Chiasm	Hymn, *Sorites*, *Ekphrasis*	Hymn, Poetry, Encomium	*Sorites*	Dialogue, allegory
Effects	Saving self and hearers	Faithful endurance, Prevent forgetfulness	Instructions for teaching in a family business	Moral change	Correction, instruction, Moral change	Educative, causes preservation of the community, discipline, maintain life	Mutual correction within the audience, casting out sin, humility	Correction, Piety, Forgiveness of sins

A PERFORMANCE THAT MATTERED

Early Christian evidence suggests that the experience of performance was different than a performance of a Greco-Roman play, letter, or story because of the people in the audience and the content of delivery. Because the audience formed around the Jesus, they remembered him and the lives of faithful figures differently. The performances reframed their memories of early Jewish ancestors, affected the listener's moral life, connected the listeners to the eyewitness and ear witness reports of Jesus, linked them with others in the community, and taught them about suffering.

From our analysis of performers and audiences in early Christian contexts, we have learned that they mattered to each other in ways that shaped their communities. The concept of Christians having an emerging *paideia* is not new. Since Werner Jaeger's 1960 lectures at Harvard,[69] we have tried to connect the world of *paideia* to the world of ancient performance. When Paul urges the Colossians to "have this [letter] read," the recitation defines their existence and their identity. Early Christian documents record performers and performances. Even what appears to be one-way communication in epistolary form from sender to receiver involves multiple layers of transmission through an amanuensis, a courier, and a lector. The writer is a recipient of communications through training, formally or informally, and alludes to the need for performance in the congregations.

The significance of performance becomes especially clear when reading the *paideia* texts. Knowing that the performances matter and the early Christian communities orient their lives around Jesus, the audiences are shaped by the gestures, figures, and memories in the performance. The Gospels and Acts reveal engaged audiences interrupting, questioning, and even retelling the stories after they are performed.

While both the early Christian performances and those of the ancient world used gestures, rhetorical figures, and memory in performance and the audiences responded appropriately by listening, gazing, interrupting, and remembering, early Christian performances shaped their audiences differently. In other words, in light of the *paideia* texts, something different is happening. The *paideia* performance texts suggest that performance *paideia* is so widespread that this becomes one of the central effects of performance, the shaping of a Christian culture.

69. Jaeger, *Christianity and Paideia*, 60.

In this *paideia,* memory is a collaborative effort among performer, listener, and God. From the early Christian audience's perspective, God remembers the audience and enables them by grace to be taught and shaped by their memories. They draw on the ancient Jewish notion that God's act of memory and forgetting enables the person to change and the community to form. The community's acts of recall, paraphrase, interruption, correction, and repetition are a mnemonic process of piety. The people listen and reframe their memories of the past. The performer recites from a trained memory and adapts to the needs of the audience. Early Christian performances view God's divine enablement of memory as part of their formation in the parenting process. They consider God to be involved through their reflections and instructions regarding some forms of suffering, as a parent disciplined a child. Instead of being formed around a society's virtues or accountability to one another, their identities are formed around one person, Jesus. Of course, this formation is of particular concern to both Hellenistic and Jewish groups for different reasons. The more the performances shape their views of Jesus, the more they differentiate themselves in their conduct and way of life.

The audiences and the performers are not limited to the elite, trained citizens. In fact, the writings reflect that the untrained had access to the performances and were also shaped in a world that is aligning itself with "there is neither Jew nor Greek, male nor female, slave nor free."

At this point, we have simply used the *paideia* texts as a lens through which to view performances. There are multiple possibilities for approaches, of course, when thinking through performance; and most of these are in the hands of the audiences and readers. Given what we know, however, we can approach the early Christian documents with a different set of questions. Interpreters are already armed with the historical-critical, source, form, narrative, and rhetorical analyses of early Christian writings. Most of these analyses approach the early Christian documents as static texts written by asking what the author meant or what the audiences expected the author to mean. The above discussion suggests we could approach the documents as texts that come alive when given to living people, the reader, and the audiences in collaboration with one another. We need a different set of questions that open different doors of interpretation. To those questions we now turn.

4

Delivering Jesus from Memory

O how foolish you are, and how slow of heart to believe all that the
prophets have declared!

Luke 24.25

IF YOU WANT TO know what mattered in performance, just watch the
audience. In the ancient world, the audience's reactions and behavior
informed the readers. The lectors were so concerned about audience response that they shaped their performances to adjust to the audience's
expectations.

In early Christian communities, lectors performed letters, biographies, apocalypses, and sermons for the community; and the audience
responded in ways that shaped who they were and how they lived. These
performances functioned as a form of *paideia:* parental instruction, education, and cultural formation for early Christian communities.

In the field of performance criticism, we lack questions to ask about
the text in order to engage the performance. Most responses are either
implied by the narrator's audience within the Gospel (the story audience),
or expected from what we know about ancient performances (the performer's audience). We need a basic set of questions to approach the static
text to open our imaginations to the performance of these narratives in
the ancient world.

As noted in the first chapter, rhetorical criticism has given us
a way to analyze the speech's outline (the critical points and moves to
understand the basic structure of the story) and the resulting potential

interpretations.[1] Historically and sociologically, we can approach the text with background information for a dramatic performance.[2] This chapter suggests a set of questions that open the mind to view audience-reader engagement based on what we read in the text and what we know of early Christian *paideia's* impact. We then apply these questions to a performance analysis of several passages in the Synoptics that the performer and the audience could have used to shape one another.

QUESTIONS FOR A PERFORMANCE ANALYSIS

Performance-based questions are much like the performers themselves, fluid and changeable. This fluidity does not fit easily into the historical-critical analyses of a text. We cannot control or quantify variables in performance. In fact, in the ancient world, this control is neither required nor realistic. Great works are not always reflected in performance, and great performances do not always result from good writing. Both require attentive audiences and trained readers. Given our dependence on those dynamics, we should approach a performance with questions rather than answers. Therefore, what questions could we ask to give us a sense of the tools a performer and audience need to achieve maximum impact? Which questions open doors for further reflection around the community's formation in performance?

Early Christian audiences' criteria are quite different from ours. Interestingly confusion, emotional outbursts, and antagonism are good responses. Debates, disagreement, and corrections are part of the process. The worst responses are distraction or apathy.

The New Testament contains 27 examples that capture attention for one reason or another. We are not sure when they became fixed in their present form; but we can assume that during the first two centuries of the church's life, they began to be heard and distributed throughout the Mediterranean world.[3] As the early communities emerged, these were heard. Based on what we know about early Christian performance, they shaped an identity to which we still respond.

1. Kennedy, *New Testament Rhetorical Criticism*, 3–5. Witherington, *New Testament Rhetoric*, 214–35.

2. Swanson, *Provoking Matthew*, 56.

3. Rhoads, "Performance as Research," 162.

We can ask several critical questions that open possibilities for an audience to see or hear:

1. Where are the lists, allusions to ancient texts, enthymemes, impersonations, and visualization? Rhetorical figures play an important part in a text's rhetorical analysis. Certain ones are frequently used in the New Testament and provide helpful analysis points. *Sorites, testimonia,* enthymemes, characterizations, and *ekphrasis* play critical parts in ancient audiences' formation.

    The lists (*sorites*) linked the eyewitnesses to a group of people who functioned as sites of memory for the community. These lists occur in the New Testament as a chain link of virtues (Rom 5; Gal 5), names in genealogies (Matthew 1; Luke 3); and faithful exemplars (Heb 11). Just as a Greco-Roman performer used monuments and battlefields to recount the history of an event, the early Christian performer used characterizations of people and memories of events as sites of memory for the group. Performances moved the audience to tears, inspired them, and shaped their imaginations.

    Hebrew scriptures, proverbs, maxims, and Jesus' sayings provided the early Christian communities necessary evidence (*testimonia*) as well as persuasive power. The audience engaged through enthymemes, open-ended stories and parables, and the rhetorical figures in the Gospels and epistles. Through enthymemes, open-ended stories, and gaps in the text, we can identify places that the audience functioned as the performer's fellow workers to arrive at conclusions.[4]

2. What are the gestures, both explicit and implicit, and what do they imply about the effect? The speeches in Acts indicate motions to the crowd as well as implicit gestures from sitting, standing, and tearing clothes that have a certain impact depending on the manner of delivery. Bodily postures and facial expressions are critical in performance. Although little evidence of these texts' dramatic portrayal exists, performers—at least in the first two centuries—called others out of the crowd or pointed at them evoking a response with gestures. All of these nonverbal tools are

---

4. Maxwell, *Hearing Between the Lines,* 160–65; Witherington III, *Letters for Hellenized Christians,* 341

at the lector's disposal.

Some of these tools might provide an opportunity to note the stage directions,[5] but it is unlikely that these alone affected the audience. There would need to be some way of understanding how these change or shape the audience differently even if the performer changed. Stage directions and cues suggest that the performer imitated/impersonated the people in the text or use gestures in some way to affect the audience. Therefore, the texts give us clues about the performance.

3.   What emotions are present in the text? Audience and performer are most likely mutually engaged in a narrative's emotional power. Through the emotions of pity, emulation, envy, and indignation, Aristotle believes the orator can reveal character (*Rhet.* 2.8–11).[6] In performance, emotions affect judgment and moral response. The performance audience brings a certain range of emotions to the setting. Especially when they are feeling persecuted or pressured (1 Peter, Hebrews, James), their emotional state provides an interesting starting point for response. The performance audience is emotionally involved and can vary their reactions depending on how the lector uses the emotions.

4.   Where is a performance audience addressed directly in the story audience? When a speaker alludes to the story audience within the Gospel with words like "Whoever has ears to hear," "As you know," "Blessed is the one who hears," the lector can exploit these allusions, treating them as an aside to the performance audience.[7] A gesture, nod, a gaze, or vocal inflections create the shift. Aristotle explains that sometimes the performer even goes onstage ahead of time to cue the audience (*Rhet.* 3.16.1417b).

5.   How does the story audience respond explicitly within the narrative? The text suggests how a reader performs to the audience. The performance audience does not have a script. When the story audience responds in the text, the performance critic does not

5. Allen, "Performance and the New Testament," in Childers and Schmit, *Performance in Preaching*, 122–30.

6. Fortenbaugh, "Aristotle on Emotions," in Fitzgerald, *Passions and Moral Progress*, 42. Kennedy calls these moods in the audience that affected judgment.

7. Shiner, *Proclaiming the Gospel*, 178.

necessarily expect the performer's audience to react the same. Aristotle clarifies this point in his analysis of rhetoric. Depending on the level of emotions within the text, the audience will respond differently. For instance, an angry audience within the story might create confidence in the performer's audience. The effect depends on whether the character described is someone intended to be imitated.

For example, the presentation of Jesus and Stephen in the Gospel of Luke might be used in different ways. Clearly Jesus turns some people off in Luke, especially when he is praying or talking to them. Others, he inspires. The presentation of Stephen also parallels the presentation of Jesus.[8] The angrier the story audience becomes the more confident and faithful the performer's audience grows.

To calm the audience's fears, a performance shows characters that are afraid. In the Gospel's storm scenes, a greater effect is achieved when the characters are more afraid. In these cases, we are obviously not seeing people imitating disciples. When the story audience grows more afraid, the performance audience becomes calm.

Even with this use of emotion, the performance audience might be dissuaded or unmoved. The opposite could and likely would happen. Paul worries about the Galatians' response to his appeal and wants to change the tone of his voice (Gal 4.20) and has difficulty communicating with the Corinthians (2 Cor 7.12) in multiple letters. An analysis might include what negative responses could be anticipated based on the performance. Some people do not grow more confident, but instead have their fears reinforced. The performer considers this variable as he reads the text, placing even greater importance on the performer's understanding of the story and performance audience.

6. What does the text help the audience remember? Memory is not memorization; memory is a process of recall, retention, paraphrase, recognition, practice, and response. *Testimonia* from Hebrew scriptures, sayings of Jesus, parables, and *chreia* are opportunities to change and reshape memories. The story world

8. As noted by Talbert and most recently Reiko Maxwell.

alludes to various memories that shape the performer's world. In this case, I am not suggesting a performer is limited to one or two versions of Jesus, or even four, as in the case of four Gospels. The Gospels catch a performance on the page, and the conventions of performance encourage the reader to elaborate from this point. The final form of the Gospels when used in performance suggests a beginning point but not a finished product. The listeners must complete the process even within the stories of the Gospels. I am proposing that these biographies offer a wide range of ways to view Jesus that left the authorial and the performer's world in awe. No one characterization of Jesus can be expected. Depending on how the lector reads him, not solely as prophet, teacher, lector, or healer, but all (and more) can be present in performance. Just as Jesus' titles and roles suggest various functions in the Gospel,[9] the New Testament performers cause people to remember Jesus in various ways. A performer does not look through the options (humorist, sage, prophet, storyteller) in Greco-Roman or Israelite portrayals to see which one might portray Jesus. Instead, the performer uses these different options depending on the need in performance, their reflection in the text, and the variety of responses the audience offers.

The collective result is a community shaped around a person's memories and the process of differentiating from former loyalties and communities. In some cases, the communities remained connected (1 Peter); in other places, they separated (Gospel of John); but in all cases, the performances are part of this explanation of identity.

7.   How does a performance change the performer? Just as Timothy's reading saves him, so the speaker's ethos plays a vital role in performance. This ethos does not center, however, on the performer's health, beauty, or family standing, but on the reader's fidelity to the way of Jesus. A reading changes the performer when reads.

8.   How does a performance affect an audience? The philosophical schools suggest a whole range of possibilities from "enlarging the soul" when a person listened to the beautiful, to modifying be-

9. Talbert, *Matthew*, 67.

havior in a person's life. All of this early Christian *paideia* created several possibilities for the audience. The performance is viewed as instruction in *paideia*. The overall effect is akin to children being disciplined by parents, receiving encouragement, reflecting on training or instruction, or learning from suffering. They grow in their understanding as people connected in community and formed by mutual bonds of affection with others through the process. A performance analysis asks how the texts achieve or eliminate this possibility for the audience. Some are turned away, others respond positively, still others debate and question. When the text is analyzed, we can expect character to be shaped in various ways: identification with Jesus, links to one another in community, retelling of stories and events to others, virtuous change of life pattern and conduct, and beneficent responses to others' needs.

DELIVERING JESUS FROM MEMORY

Performing the Gospel accounts of Jesus' life raises different questions about the text than the traditional historical-critical questions about the memories of Jesus and their authenticity. We have not tried to reconstruct the memories of sayings that led to a performance of the Gospels.[10] While interesting from the historians' viewpoint in reconstructing the various witnesses to Jesus' life, the Gospels in their final form were delivered to audiences that heard Jesus' life and the lives of those around Jesus from their perspectives. As James Dunn suggested, these were not layers of data or recollections but performances somewhere between rote memorization and reminiscences.[11] This performance was an act of commemoration where storytelling, performance, and interaction come together as part of community emulation. They imitate each other telling and retelling the stories.[12] In so doing, the performances changed their memories of him and each other, created an identity around him and the communities to whom the Gospels were performed, inspired the stories to be told,

---

10. For examples for those who do, read Allison, *Constructing Jesus*, 17–20; and Bauckham, *Jesus and the Eyewitnesses*, 264–89.

11. Dunn, *Jesus Remembered*, 249.

12. White, *Scripting Jesus*, 102.

enlarged their souls, and created debates within the communities about the practices and purposes of early Christians going forward.

Thus far, this book has proposed that for the early audience, the performance of the text mattered. When looking at performances of the Gospels, we want to anticipate the likely effect a performance of the stories about and around Jesus had on early listeners. To do so, we need to analyze the text using the questions we proposed and apply these to a performance of Jesus.

PERFORMANCE ANALYSIS

The performance process mattered to the audience. We begin with the structure of the text, the gestures, and obvious vocal inflection. In ancient performance analysis, however, especially of Gospels, we examine speeches and stories within a larger work. We pay attention to the way the audience within the Gospel responded and the likely responses an ancient performance audience has. The rhetorical handbooks emphasize that the performer could use emotions in various ways depending on the setting and the audience. The audience interacts with the performer, fills in gaps, and participates through applause, silence, listening, correction, retention, paraphrase, and retelling.

This means, of course, that each audience is affected differently. Some audiences are moved, others not so much. Some audiences identify with the characters, and others are turned away. The text gives us some clues to the auditors' expectations, and the ancient world's literature provides a good resource connecting the emotions of the story and the likely performance audience responses. Speakers can vary the performance from place to place. Given what we read in the text, we can expect something similar to this in early Christian audiences. When the same conventions are in the text, we have clues to anticipate how an audience is probably affected. The entire process involves forming a community around Jesus in various ways. There is no one-size-fits-all model of performance or formation. The process, however, creates the beginning of very good news.

SEEING EACH OTHER AS BLESSED: MATTHEW 5.1–11

The opening of the Sermon on the Mount marks a significant moment in Matthew. Jesus is portrayed as an orator-teacher: "he opened his mouth" (Matthew 5:2) with a crowd of followers all of whom are drawn to his teaching either by selection or by magnetism.[13] The sermon functions as deliberative rhetoric, teaching people how to see differently[14], and opens with an encomium of the blessed person's character. The nature of the behavior, of course, is a matter of great debate. Performance criticism suggests that with the encomium, these are the kinds of characteristics an orator sees in his audience and wants to draw out of them.

The only gesture noted is the posture of a seated teacher. The pose reflects the beginning of the speech and anticipates that eventually he will vary his posture and stand (Matt 6:5; Quintilian *Inst. Or.* 11.3.44).

The Beatitudes' opening lines function as an exordium for the speech (vs. 1–12). The gesture likely would have been the one used to alert an audience that the orator is speaking (Quintilian *Inst. Or.* 11.3.96–100)—the index finger and third finger extended, the thumb pointing upward, and the fourth and fifth fingers folded into the hand.

The passage uses the figure of the *anaphora*, repetition of the first word of each sentence in the poem, "Blessed," emphasizing the words to follow and impressing the listeners (*Inst.* 9.3.30). This *anaphora* is also a *sorites* of the qualities that define the blessed life. As Aristotle notes, in encomium, the speaker praises a person for qualities that he wants him to develop or that a person thinks he already has developed (*Rhet.* 1.9.5 1368a). This emphasis fits the Roman world's personal achievement toward character for healthy, male, elites.

Matthew's audience hears important differences between the Mediterranean world and Jesus' blessing. Unlike the encomium designed to praise a person for qualities he has or can develop, the performance offers a new understanding of character. They hear the way they are viewed by Jesus as the orator. God takes the initiative first to provide these rewards.[15] The listener's character is highlighted and explained.[16] They hear praise heaped upon them for qualities they may not realize or know they

13. Talbert, *Reading the Sermon on the Mount*, 12.

14. Keener, *Matthew*, 161.

15. Keener, *Matthew*, 167.

16. Turner, *Matthew*, 149.

possess. The listener is not dependent on his education, skills, or value to achieve this position. The promise and blessing are gifts of grace.[17]

The emotion intensifies with the shift from third- to second-person plural in verse 11: "Blessed are you." The rhetorical effect is significant because the performer shifts vocal inflection and intensity in his voice. Longinus notes the importance of the shift from third person to second in performance: "Similarly the change of person makes for a sense of involvement in the struggle and often gives the audience the opinion that it is embroiled in the middle of dangers" (*[Subl.]* 26.1). This effect "turns the sense of hearing into the sense of sight" (26.2).

A gesture signifies that the speaker directs the statement to the entire group. The performance audience is blessed now and is a recipient of an eschatological promise that their lives fulfill. This is performative language,[18] but the performance is not individualistic. Our study of performances sheds light on group identity. The performance audience learns who they are as well as the person with whom they identify. They are not victims or heroes. They are learners (disciples), students being trained (*paideia*) to see the world through the eyes of Jesus as teacher-orator.

Using the language and gesture of blessing, the experience recalls two blessing scenes from the Hebrew scripture. The first is parents blessing children through Abraham, Isaac, and Jacob. The listeners bear the name and blessing of Jesus and honor him with their lives.

The second is the blessing from the wisdom tradition as parents teach wise instruction to children (Psalm 1; Proverbs 3).[19] In the case of the beatitudes, the experiences of mercy, persecution, and suffering are part of the curriculum of instruction.[20]

They are known as people whom God has blessed. They share this corporate identity with others around Jesus. Because he sees them this way, and announces these characteristics before they see them in each other, much like Aristotle suggested, they begin to see themselves with these qualities that shape and form them as part of the community (Aristotle).

---

17. Talbert, *Matthew*, 80.

18. Boring, "*Matthew*," 179.

19. Witherington, *Matthew*, 120.

20. Keener, *Matthew*, 172.

Just as Plutarch anticipates, groups form around a figure. In the ancient world, the competitive nature of *paideia* prevents authentic relationships. Friendships are based on mutually beneficial ties to one another in community.

In this case, the early Christians begin to see each other in ways that make this identity possible to shape the community life in Matthew. This group functions more like the brotherhood, and now sisterhood, of 4 Maccabees. The blessings and experiences described in the beatitudes bring them together to learn and shape their lives around Jesus. The performance of the Beatitudes reveals that their persecution and suffering taught them the discipline of being formed around Christ in *paideia*. The communal *sorites* of people repeated through the *anaphora* draws people together. The list links them with each other. Here the Beatitudes enact a kingdom that is with us, seeing one another in light of the suffering and characteristics that the community faces together (4 Macc. 10.20; 13.22; 16.19; 17.9–10 LXX; Heb. 11–12).

LAUGHING AT PIETY: MATTHEW 6.5–23

Another section of the Sermon on the Mount uses humor through the mannerisms and vocal inflection of a stock character (*ethopoeia*) to disarm the skeptics, expose the folly of public religious practices, and reveal the truth of spiritual practices. In this section, the audience anticipates the use of humor and wit. We look first at the story audience and then the performance audience.

Cicero teaches that humor is an appropriate tactic in a speech (Cic. *De Or.* 2.57.270–271). Humor exposes the truth in a situation (2.61.252; 2.66.264) and arouses laughter (2.52.254) and wonder (2.52.254). A humorous speech should have "dissimilar characters, severity, gentleness, hope, fear, suspicion, desire, dissimilation, error, pity, change of fortune, unlooked-for disaster, sudden joy, and a happy ending to the affair" (*Inv.* 1.27 [King, LCL]).

> The things most easily ridiculed are those which call for neither strong disgust nor the deepest sympathy. This is why all laughing-matters are found among those blemishes noticeable in the conduct of people who are neither objects of general esteem nor yet full of misery and no apparently merely fit to be hurried off to

execution for their crimes; and these blemishes if deftly handled, raise laughter. (*De Or.* 2.59.238 [Sutton, LCL]; cf. 2.67.269)

Humorous speeches employ stock themes of braggarts, the pompous, the thieving, the conniving, and the greedy. To find humor grammatically, one looks for sustained metaphors, alliteration, repeated words, and ideas.[21] To achieve the effect, the orator "borrows a suspicion" of mimicry so that "the hearer may imagine more than meets the eye" (Cicero *De Or.* 2.49.242).

This section of the Sermon on the Mount fits this humorous presentation. The passage uses the stock theme of hypocrites as braggarts and pompous actors in all forms of religions. The text repeats words such as "alms," "prayer," and "fasting." The reader performs an *ethopeia* of hypocrites. The generic term indicates they are neither esteemed nor maligned, but are familiar to the population. Jesus avoids characterizing the Pharisees this way in the speech.[22] Anyone can be a hypocrite. Some in the story audience may recognize their own faults or overemphasis of the issues addressed. These are familiar themes that any devoted religious person, whether Jew or Gentile, would have understood. Many give alms in the temple to be recognized, stand on street corners to pray, and look haggard when fasting.

The performer exposes the blemishes in religious piety, whether Greco-Roman or Jewish, with "graphic word pictures"[23] and hyperbole but does not subject these blemishes to extreme ridicule. The hyperboles are not designed to malign the Pharisees; instead, they reveal the speaker's character. The trumpet blowing during almsgiving is not known in the ancient world but may have been used as a metaphor (Dem. *Or.* 25.90; Achilles Tatius 8.10.10; Dio Chrys. *Or.* 8.2; Cicero, *Fam.* 16.21.2; Juvenal 14.152)[24] or could have referred to trumpet-shaped chests near the temple. The hyperbole functions the same either way. Jest and humor are mirrors in which the people can see their behavior.

The performance reinforces the simplicity and secrecy of the disciple's practices. The reduplication (*conduplicatio*) of the secretive actions and the fact "that your heavenly Father who sees what is done in secret

21. Hughes, "Comedy," 193.

22. Turner, *Matthew*, 184.

23. Keener, *Matthew*, 238.

24. Nolland, *Matthew*, 274.

will reward you" open up an imaginative, symbolic world that calls the listener to laugh at himself and focus on compassion.[25] Creating a deep impression on the hearer, this figure inflicts a wound on the opposition, and in this case amplifies the humorous effect (*Rhet. Her.* 4.28.38).

The example of the model prayer (6.9–13) functions as a digression, a way of softening even further the humorous parody of the hypocrites (Quint. *Inst.* 4.3.9–11; 9.1.28–35)[26]:

> We may employ digressions and then after thus delighting our audience, make a neat and elegant return to our main theme. We may set forth in advance what we propose to say, mark off the topics already treated from those who which are to follow, return to our point, repeat and draw our formal . . ." (9.1.28) "These are the various devices for the embellishment of our style . . ." (35)

The digression highlights the simplicity of the praying disciple's actions as opposed to the hypocrite's public behavior. Just as one should give secretively, so he uses humorous hyperbole to amplify his point about prayer.[27]

The disciple does not worry about things like clothes, even when he is without them. God not only provides for people; God provides when people are without what they need. Matthew 6.8 parallels 6.33–34.[28] No one can add a single hour to his life by worrying either about today's or tomorrow's needs.[29] Here the *catechresis*, "single hour," emphasizes the futility of worry (Quint. *Inst.* 8.2.6; 8.6.34–36; *Rhet. Her.* 4.33.45).[30] The hypocrites' extreme acts of piety blind them to what they should be most concerned about—seeking God's kingdom and righteousness. This point is emphasized through the personification of tomorrow: "Tomorrow will worry about itself" (Matt 6.34; Quint. *Inst.* 9.2.36; *Rhet. Her.* 4.53.66).[31]

In performance, Jesus' *ethopeia* of the hypocrites functions as *prosōpopoiia* for the lector. We have a double impersonation—a characterization of Jesus characterizing hypocrites. We can imagine multiple options for the performer and the audience. At one level, they are

---

25. Ibid., 276.

26. Cf. Cicero *Orator* 39.134; *de Or.* 3.53.201; and *de Or.* 2.2.261.

27. Keener, *Matthew,* 211.

28. Ibid., 236.

29. Nolland, *Matthew,* 316.

30. Keener, *Matthew,* 237.

31. Ibid., 238.

still learning who Jesus is. The hyperboles and humor further open the audience's eyes. The impersonation reveals Jesus' connection with the hypocrites. The orator impersonates others who understand the content and the topic. The gestures and language have to fit the person who is performing (Quint. *Inst.* 9.2.37; 3.8.51). The speech has to be fitting, suitable to the one doing the impersonation. The performance suggests that Jesus has close contact and was, therefore, familiar with hypocrites.

The language of hypocrites/actors suggests another level of performance, much like actors on the stage. We have already seen the mirror effect of the lector. The moral figure to be imitated functions as a mirror on which to gaze and reflect, resulting in progress and change. In this case, the lector functions as a mirror for the performance audience. He acts on stage in ways so that the person can see himself in overly dramatic, humorous ways, motivating a return to the simple life. Much like a character in a play, stock figures are used to lighten the mood, evoke laughter from the audience, and drive home the point. The proud and arrogant, especially historical figures, are among the characters that speakers often imitate to evoke laughter from a crowd (Quint. *Inst.* 3.8.51). Speakers who want to imitate others humorously exaggerate their gestures, make strange faces, and speak loudly.

Religious men placed scraps of manuscripts in boxes called phylacteries and strapped them to their forehead and forearm. In their view, they were obeying the command from Leviticus that one should keep the word of God close to the head and heart. The tassels were the long strands on the sleeves and bottom of garments worn by religious teachers. According to Matthew, they not only wore the attire, but wore them to the extreme. As a result, their appearance was off-putting and intimidating and kept them from addressing matters significant to the hearer. Their clothes provided fodder for anyone imitating these people. Scribes and Pharisees wore clothes that marked them distinctively, much like an actor in the theater. They performed as religious actors wearing an arrogant mask. They gave their alms in such a way so that others will applaud their accomplishments.

The performance is not about the hypocrite but about the listener. This theme is clarified in Matthew 23 when the lector impersonates Jesus' discussion of the Pharisees with their long robes, which symbolizes their dysfunction. In Matthew 23.5, the scribes and Pharisees "do all their deeds to be seen by men; they make the phylacteries broad and their fringes long, and they love the place of honor at feasts and the best seats in the synagogues."

This imitation of Pharisees and scribes makes impersonation quite personal.[32] The actor's gestures pointing out the posture of prayer, the disfigured face, and the Gentiles' frenetic pace are all appropriate here, much like those of an actor donning a tragic mask or running around the Greco-Roman theater. As Amy Richlin observed, simple rapid movement often accompanies a humorous speech to evoke laughter from the audience.[33]

Words in the text give clues to how this section can be read. Because Jesus is poking fun at the Pharisees' outward actions, a person can imagine the nonverbal behavior used to parody them: hands upraised to imitate their prayers, disfigured facial expressions to imitate their fasting habits, and exaggerated gestures that evoke laughter.

Because the actors miss the basics of religion, a person should beware of people performing religious functions publicly. Instead, he should imitate Jesus and follow his instructions in the ways described in 6:25–7:23. This section of the sermon on the mount is a humorous mirror designed for story and performance audience to cause internal reflection on one's public religious practices.

CONFIDENCE IN AN ANGRY JESUS: MARK 3.1–6

Mark's Gospel lends itself to performance and is most frequently analyzed in performance criticism. I discuss the significance of two passages in light of ancient performance.

The first is a *chreia* from Mark 3, a story about the life of Jesus that reveals his character[34] using both his speech and action (Theon *Progymnasmata* 98–99 [Kennedy, 16–17]; Hermogenes *Progymnasmata* 7–8 [Kennedy, 76–77]). The scene occurs immediately following another controversy about the Sabbath at the end of Mark 2 and prior to his teaching ministry in Galilee. In this scene, Jesus uses words rhetorically to heal a man with a withered hand. While another version of this

---

32. Witherington, *New Testament Rhetoric*, 132.
33. Richlin, "Gender and Rhetoric," 95.
34. Witherington, *Mark*, 133.

story is also found in Matthew 12.9–14 and Luke 6.6–11[35], only Mark describes Jesus' emotional state as angry. This aspect of Jesus' character is rarely mentioned. The only other time we get the sense of indignation is at Lazarus' tomb in John 11 and in Mark 11.11 when Jesus overturns the tables in the temple.

Jesus challenges the story audience's memories of Sabbath practices with a rhetorical question (3.4), echoing Deuteronomy 30.15 LXX[36]: How are Sabbath laws to be applied to people with physical conditions? The Sabbath did not permit harming or killing others.[37] The audience is silent (3.4), and he responds to their silence with anger. In this controversy over the Sabbath, the occasion becomes a reason for the Pharisees to plot against Jesus and for the Herodians to maintain their political status quo. Ironically, those who forbid work on the Sabbath begin to plot to harm Jesus. The one who restores life to a man who does not volunteer for healing now begins a journey toward a certain end.[38] The story audience is divided, as one would expect, over the "good word" spoken on the Sabbath.

How could a performance audience respond in light of the divided story audience? The *chreia* are practiced in the rhetorical schools in various ways, changing subjects, actions. and words around the central theme to reveal character. The passage uses a connective *kai* eight times. This occurrence is not a defect in the text[39] but a "reduplication" (*conduplicatio*), "the purpose of amplification or appeal to pity . . . The reiteration of the same word makes a deep impression upon the hearer and inflicts a major wound upon the opposition—as if a weapon should repeatedly pierce the same part of the body" (*Rhet. Her.* 4.28.38–39).

Most commentators regard Jesus' anger as an expression of his righteous indignation toward the issue,[40] compassion toward the Pharisees' hard hearts,[41] an editorial change to the original story,[42] or a part of the anger psychologically that comes with grief. When read in light of performance, anger is a significant emotion used by a trained orator. Recall

35. All three passages are omitted in the lectionary.
36. France, *Mark*, 150.
37. Witherington, *Mark*, 135.
38. Ibid., 136.
39. Culpepper, *Mark*, 98.
40. Garland, *Mark*, 108; Witherington, *Mark*, 136.
41. Culpepper, *Mark*, 108.
42. Guelich, *Mark 1–8:26*, 137.

that Aristotle notes that anger is one of four emotions (pity, indignation, envy, and zeal or emulation) that an orator uses to reveal the character of a virtuous person. An audience appreciates and admires anger in certain people. If the figure is a person to be emulated, the listener gains confidence when they see and hear of his indignation (Aristotle *Rhet.* 2.5.1383a.15). In light of the convention, a performance audience gains confidence in Jesus' ability to address the controversies over the Sabbath, dietary laws, and hospitality that are part of religious life.

Mark employs a range of emotions throughout the Gospel.[43] In performance, the reader characterizes this anger with a clenched hand or places a hand on his breast (Quint. *Inst.* 11.3.104) and alters his voice to be shrill, hasty (Cicero *De Or.* 3.58.217), fierce, harsh, or intense (*Inst.* 11.3.63; 6.2.27–28). We are not sure how the story audience viewed the man, but a performance reading suggests that the performer's audience pities the man with the withered hand and empathizes with Jesus' anger toward the religious leadership. The result is an increased confidence in Jesus because of his mistreatment on the Sabbath:

> Anger is a confident thing, and to be wronged rather than to do wrong is productive of anger, but the divine is supposed to come to the aid of those who are wronged. And [people feel confident] when, laying hands to some task, they think they are not likely to suffer [now] or will succeed. (*Rhet.* 2.5.21–22 1383b [Kennedy])

The reading affects the performance audience's memory of Sabbath law. Jesus can heal with a spoken word without violating a rule. Through the power of this word spoken in performance, their memories of Sabbath laws have been changed just as the man with the withered hand is now whole. Their minds are made whole by a performance of Jesus. By overhearing the dialogue with Jesus, the Pharisees, the Herodians, and the man with the withered (now restored) hand, their confidence grows in the one who heals through the power of spoken words. Something is happening for the audience. They learn that Jesus does not violate Sabbath law but restores life to a man who does not need to wait another day for healing.[44] The word and wisdom of Jesus become a matter of time and timing.[45] The word spoken at the right time provides new and renewed

---

43. Shiner, *Proclaiming the Gospel,* 71.
44. Garland, *Mark,* 109.
45. Witherington, *Mark,* 138.

confidence in Jesus and a way to motivate the audience to take action toward the one who offers healing even on days their traditions tell them to avoid breaking laws.

In performance the *chreia* functions as a lesson about another way to keep the Sabbath (Mark 2:23–3:6). Already the dialogue with the Pharisees confronts a misuse of Sabbath teaching. The question for the performance audience is whether the synagogue can be an appropriate venue for good deeds as well as good teaching. In performance, the use of the synagogue on the Sabbath is an appropriate venue for both, especially when one is being taught like students in the school of Jesus. Just as the local synagogue is the place of reading, instruction, and formation for people in the culture of middle Judaism, so the performance of Jesus shapes the *paideia* of early followers of Jesus' way. Good deeds accompany good thoughts, and sometimes they happen in the midst of the discussion. A performance of Jesus demonstrates a way that went beyond reading and discussion to audience participation and change. The religious leadership uses the Sabbath to avoid doing good works. Now the audience hears a word that teaches them how to use the synagogue (and other places of reading) to perform good deeds.

When performed, Jesus' character carries a powerful set of emotions that likely draws on the sense of injustice from the audience and builds confidence in the character who shares their anger. Their confidence in Jesus rises and gives them courage as they face the realities of Sabbath observances, physical deformities, and political instability in their world.

THE POWER OF A SECRET: HIDDEN MEANING IN MARK 4

The Gospel of Mark provides places where the audience can be included in the performance whether through direct address ("Let the reader understand" 13:14), translations of foreign words (5:41; 7:34; 14:36; 15:22; 15:34), or third-person comments ("Let one who has ears to hear" (4:9). They mark places where the story world crosses the boundaries into the performer's world.[46]

Audience inclusion is common in the ancient world, but the convention had a certain effect. To achieve a sense of liveliness, surprise, and delight, and to allow the hearer to instruct himself the orator could use

46. Shiner, *Proclaiming the Gospel,* 178.

metaphors, hidden meanings, and riddles. (Aristotle *Rhet.* 3.2.5 1405b).
Hidden meanings in performance affect the listener as well. The hidden
meaning is left for the hearer to discover (Quint. *Inst.* 9.2.65), and the
performer leaves time for the listener to discover the meaning.

> For thus the judge will be led to seek out the secret which he would
> not perhaps believe if he heard it openly stated, and to believe in
> that which he thinks he has found out for himself. In doing this
> we shall find emotional appeals, hesitation and words broken by
> silences most effective (9.2.71).

Allegories (Quint. *Inst.* 8.6.58) and fables (Theon *Progymnasmata*
74), often told with a certain sense of obscurity, achieve the same kind
of effect as riddles. They cause their listeners to seek the hidden meaning and in turn receive instruction. The images in the metaphors and
riddles place images before the listener's eyes, creating liveliness and surprise (*Rhet.* 3.11.1–3) as the listener discovers the meaning. Even though
Quintilian warns against the excessive use of riddles, veiled meanings and
metaphors involved the audience in the mystery.

The imagery of soil and seed in the allegory has a particular effect
on the mind, heart, or soul. Different comparisons have different effects
on the audience. A comparison like the one involving the soil is used
to argue that the mind requires cultivation, "which if neglected produces thorns and thickets, but if cultivated will bear fruit" (Quint. *Inst.*
5.11.24). Even fertile soil requires cultivation to produce fruit (Cicero
Tusc. Discp. 2.13).

In addition to what we already know about Mark 4, the parable of the
sower provides a helpful example of the performance's role when dealing
with the issues of revealing and concealing,[47] explaining, drawing people
in, and involving the audience. Mark's version provides enough words to
involve the audience, "Listen!" (4.3) "Let him who has ears to hear . . ."
(4.9).[48] The emphasis in the parable and the allegorical interpretation is
framed by appeals to an audience to listen and understand. Despite interpreters' best attempts to demonstrate that the parables prevent understanding, quite the opposite happens in performance. This parable is also
a riddle.[49] The purpose of allegories, riddles, and enigmas are designed

---

47. Wire, *Mark Composed in Performance*, 156–57.

48. Shiner, *Proclaiming the Gospel*, 177–78; Thatcher, *Jesus the Riddler*, 39.

49. France, *Mark*, 188.

to delight the audience and to cultivate understanding (Aristotle *Rhet.* 2.20.1ff; 3.17.5; Quint. *Inst.* 3.8.34; 5.11.22–30; 8.3.74–75).

Interpreters have struggled to hold both the parable and the allegorical interpretation in one unit.[50] A reading in performance achieves this unity because the Gospel preserves both parts together. The listener interprets the command to listen as an invitation to the audience as well.

When read in light of performance, the interpretation functions to cultivate the disciples' minds, inviting more questions and response. They are drawn in by Jesus' urge to listen (Mark 4.3, 9)[51] and are puzzled, as one would expect, by the parable and the interpretation from Isaiah. The need for further explanation is part of the process of cultivating their hearts and those listening.

They respond with more questions. Two enigmas are present. First, Jesus uses a *testimonia* from Isaiah 6.9–10 that is also a popular maxim from the ancient world used to explain dullness or obduracy (4 Ezra 10.35; Wis. 4.15; Demostehenes *Against Aristogeiton* 1.89; Lucian *Dialogues of the Sea-Gods* 4; Aeschylus *Agamemnon* 1621–624; Plutarch *[Lib. ed.]* 18 Moralia 13E). The second enigma is the referent in the allegorical interpretation of the parable. The seed is both the word and the soils.

First, we look at the *testimonia*. Isaiah *testimonia* puzzles the disciples because teaching in parables results for some in dullness or in obduracy to the message.

> To you has been given the secret of the kingdom of God; but for those outside, everything comes in parables in order that 'they may indeed look but not perceive, and may indeed listen, but not understand; so that they may not turn again and be forgiven.' (Mark 4.11–12)

One option in performance is to read the prophecy ironically with appropriate gestures and vocal inflection. Mark 4.12 can be read, "The last thing they would want is to turn and have their sins forgiven!"[52]

---

50. For instance, Thatcher notes that this parable is a riddle and does not make sense without Jesus' interpretation. In order to explain the riddle, he says that "Jesus' private commentary on the parable, which appears in verses 14–20, was most likely not given until later on in the story, somewhere between verses 34 and 35. Mark has simply put the events out of order for stylistic reasons." Thatcher, *Jesus the Riddler,* 38.

51. Garland, *Mark,* 109.

52. France, *Mark.* 200.

Another option in performance is to assume that this mystery only delights the hearers more in the story audience and the performance audience. Another part of the secret (*musterion*) is cultivating their hearts, and they are left wondering how the various soils will respond.

How can those inside receive and some of those outside not? The answer comes in the second enigma, the riddle of the mysterious seed. This seed functions grammatically as both the seed and the soil (4.14–20). The seed cultivates their hearts, clears out the thorns and thickets, and apparently changes the soil from one kind to another. Because a field requires cultivation, so does a soul (Cicero *Tusc. Disp.* 2.13), through instruction.

The performance of the parable cultivates the ears of the disciples. Jesus is a highly distinctive teacher who evokes questions and responses that are a part of the presentation. The disciples need long-term teaching and receptiveness in their hearts. They are curious but need further cultivation.[53] In this case, the Isaiah text and allegory function as the reason for educating the disciples and anyone else who is receptive. The results may depend on the condition of the recipients and their receptiveness to the seed,[54] but these conditions can be changed by the performance. A performance opens the possibility that a listener will not always have one kind of soil. Instead, the eager listener with questions is actually being cultivated by the allegorical interpretation, questions, and response. As the performer includes the audience, their minds are cultivated further by the word.

A performance is not enough. The performer needs the audience. In this case, Jesus as the teacher needs people who not only listen but also listen willingly.[55] The parable with the allegory is an exercise in performance criticism because of the importance of the audience within the Gospel as well as those watching the Gospel being performed. The effect is the same. Instead of reading Isaiah as a message that closes off the conversation with the word of God, the performance reframes Isaiah as an invitation to draw curious listeners closer.

This performance could change how we read, understand, or perform characterizations of the disciples. Rather than stumbling bumbling idiots where confusion is a source of ignorance, confused by the parables

53. Ibid., 195, 204.
54. Witherington, *Mark*, 198.
55. France, *Mark*, 205.

or conversations with Jesus,[56] they instead are in the process of being trained and taught how to train and teach others. Their *paideia*, if you will, is the process of the deep mysterious realm of the parables, sometimes confusing, often debatable, but forever formational to those who want to know more.

The mysterious nature of the teaching and the enigma of both listener and seed as the same "word" motivate the quest for insight. The enigmas draw the listener closer to the nature of disciples who, by their very role, ask many questions. They may not understand, but they are very interested and inquisitive. Surprised and delighted, they discover that the best method of instruction for this teacher is disciples who can learn to discover the solutions themselves.

Parables and other mysteries are more than puzzles to be solved or decoded. They are rhetorical figures that draw the story and performance audiences closer. Their secrecy makes the information privileged but not incomprehensible.[57] Even when solved, parables are to be argued, debated, questioned, and engaged at several levels with a series of new questions. In the process, the hearts of those who want to listen are further cultivated.

GAZING AT A MIRROR: AUDIENCE REACTION IN LUKE 4.16–30

In the Gospel of Luke, Jesus' first performance in a synagogue provides a case study of audience reaction as well as performance criticism. How can an audience move from a reaction of awe and pleasure to wrath? What effect does this kind of scene have on the performance audience?

First, we examine the story audience. Luke 4's recitation and interpretation in the Nazareth synagogue fit the conventions of recitation in the following settings: Greco-Roman (Horace *Sat.* 1.9.23–25; Ovid *Ars* 3.345–346; Pliny *Ep* 34.1–2; Nepos *Atticus* 14.1; Gellius 2.22.1; (Suet. *Vita Virg.* 33; Pliny *Ep.* 5.3), Hellenistic Jewish (Philo *Prob.* 80–83; *QE* 2.34), the Qumran community (1 QS 6.7–8; CD 13.2–4) and early Christian (Acts 15; 1 Cor. 10.21). In each, a lector reads, and the audience responds

56. Beavis suggests they function for Mark's audience as examples of "what not to do." Beavis, *Mark's Audience*, 182.

57. France, *Mark.* 196.

either positively or negatively. The reader interacts with the audience or anticipates some response or correction during the reading.

Luke has provided the significant rhetorical phrase "from his mouth" (4.22) indicating not only Jesus' presence as a wisdom teacher (Sirach 51.23–28; Deut 8.3 Isaiah 50.4; 55.11 LXX) but also the rhetorical connection to one of the organs associated with speech, retelling, and memory (Philo *Det.* 12.40; Xenophon *On Symposium* 3.5–6; Plato *Thaetetus* 143a).

In this case, Jesus reads paraphrases of Isaiah 61.1 and 58.6 LXX. He adds an infinitive to Isaiah 58.6 LXX: to bring good news, to proclaim, to let go free, and to proclaim. The proclamation is asserted as the focus of the work. From the perspective of performance, this kind of paraphrase fits the rhetorical conventions of memory. Whether or not Luke "carefully chose and arranged the elements,"[58] in performance a lector can use memory to paraphrase texts and weave them together.

The people gaze at him. The theme of the gaze is more significant in Acts than in Luke (Luke 22.56; Acts 1.10; 3.4,12; 6.15; 7.55; 10.4; 11.6; 13.9; 14.9; 23.1).[59] From what we have seen, the audience's reaction to a gaze is more than "tense expectancy."[60] Jesus as the lector becomes a mirror for the people to look at and reflect upon themselves. Jesus places himself in the position of a prophetic moral figure of his time. The Isaiah text represents the character of the speaker and the content of his ministry.[61] During the gaze, he assumes the posture of a teacher (like Matthew 5) and "begins" to say to them "Today this scripture is fulfilled," indicating that he is not only a person to admire but also a person who provides an example, much like a Father shows his son how to behave (Plutarch *[Lib. ed.]* 20).

The story audience thinks of him as the son of Joseph but not quite the "son of God" (Luke 3.23–38).[62] They cannot imagine that a neighbor could fulfill the position that Luke has placed Jesus in.[63] They are amazed

58. Culpepper, *Luke*, 105.

59. Johnson, *Luke,* 81.

60. Marshall, *Luke,* 185; Bock, *Luke,* 1:412.

61. Johnson, *Luke,* 81.

62. Culpepper, Luke, 106.

63. Bock, *Luke,* 1.415

at his ability to speak[64] with the "gracious words" that "come from his mouth." This is the extent of their admiration.

Jesus, however, is not presented as an admirable speaker or teacher but a prophetic mirror. In the ancient world, orators spoke frankly to audiences using proverbs (*testimonia* and maxims), to motivate people to examine themselves, especially those who knew the speaker and his character well and who could be brought to "their sober senses." If an audience responds with jealousy or envy, the speaker uses their reaction to motivate them further. From a rhetorical perspective, spite merely awakens their attention in performance. (Plutarch *Adult. Amic.* 32–33 Mor. 71–72)

Jesus speaks frankly to the hometown crowd with a proverb: "Doctor, cure yourself." He recalls Elijah and Elisha stories from their history they were not prepared to address. Their response is much like the people Aristotle described. They are envious toward a neighbor whose success reproaches the audience (*Rhet.* 2.10 1388a15). As Seneca suggests, an envious audience can change their reactions if the orator holds their attention uses maxims to drive home his point (Seneca *Ep.* 2.35.6–2.35.4; Seneca *Ep.* 108.8–12). Crowds can change their behavior, especially if what they are seeing does not match what they wanted to see in themselves. Even if they come for entertainment or unprepared to change, the crowd can still be moved. In most cases, the anger or hostility provokes imitation of the speaker by the audience and enlarges their view of his character.

Jesus provokes his hometown crowd with a retort,[65] a response that does not sit well with a modern picture of Jesus,[66] but does fit the conventions of rhetoric when an orator attempts to motivate the audience to change. A prophet, especially one paraphrasing Isaiah 58, rebukes as much as encourages crowds.[67] The story audience rejects the invitation and attempts to kill Jesus, who narrowly escapes.

Wrath, envy, and anger directed at a figure to be emulated do not necessarily close off the story audience forever. The synagogue is filled with wrath, but the crowd's response is not final. Jesus is able to escape through the crowd, leaving room for change. Their wrath, much like those

---

64. Vinson, *Luke*, 122; Bock, *Luke*, 1:414.

65. Bovon, *Luke*, 1:155; Nolland, *Luke 1–9:20*, 199.

66. Vinson, *Luke*, 123.

67. Bock, *Luke*, 1:406.

angered at what they see in themselves or envious of the person, provides the chance to change later (Plutarch *Rect. rat. aud.* 6 *Mor.* 38E).

How does a performance audience of the Gospel respond to this scene? From the performance perspective, the scene contains all the elements of a pleasant experience for the audience: movement, memory, anger, jealousy, and a narrow escape at the end (*Rhet.* 1.11 1370b-1371b10).[68]

Hearing a performance of this scene, the audience considers several choices, much like those addressed in Plutarch's lectures, Seneca's discussion of anger, and Hebrews' sermon to gaze on Jesus (Heb. 12:2). They can choose Jesus as a figure to be emulated and use the lector as a mirror to gaze reflectively at their condition, or they can choose the response of the crowd and become further enraged. Depending on how the lector performs the crowd's reaction, the performance audience can react with greater horror and indignation at Jesus' opponents. The performance reveals the character of Jesus as well as the lack of character in the crowd. (Aristotle *Rhet.* 1395a 5-10). They can also cause a person to receive these words as gifts of grace and recognize as the gift of frank speech and correction (Plutarch *Rect. rat. aud.* 5 *Mor.* 38E).

As a performer, the reader stands as a mirror between the text and the audience. The performer's life became the natural mirror for them to gaze upon themselves, compare themselves to the story, and reflect on their behavior in light of the crowd's response. By asking how the people react to Jesus, they can see themselves in the story and evaluate their responses.

The performer has to choose how to read Jesus' retort. One likely possibility is humor. A quick witty response to a question, accusation, or statement using a proverb was a form of rhetorical raillery. In response the audience laughs. As Cicero notes,

> The things most easily ridiculed are those which call for neither strong disgust nor the deepest sympathy. This is why all laughing-matters are found among blemishes noticeable in the conduct of people who are neither objects of general esteem nor yet full of misery and not apparently merely fit to be hurried off to execution for their crimes; and these blemishes, if deftly handled, raise laughter (*De Or.* 2.59.238 [Sutton, LCL]; cf. 2.67.269)

---

68. "Dramatic turns of fortune and hairbreadth escapes from perils are pleasant, because we feel all such things are wonderful" (1371b10).

In performance, the story in Nazareth functions as a way to demonstrate the character of Jesus' ministry as well as to cause a person to examine his response in light of Jesus' message. Using the memory of Elijah and Elisha, the listeners in performance examine their motives, passions, anger, and pay attention to the presence of the prophet in their midst. When Elijah, Elisha, and Jesus are around, they announce a prophetic message; but widows are not fed.[69] The memory of these characters causes the individual and community to assess their work in light of Jesus' announcement and challenge. Their view of Jesus' character grows as they marvel at not only his gracious words but also his frank speech given as a rebuke and correction for those he knows best. As he is rejected, so they anticipate similar rejection; but that is the nature of the ministry of the spirit and the prophet.

VISUAL RECOGNITION: LUKE 24.13–35

The scene on the road to Emmaus provides an example of a performance of Jesus when listeners moved from blindness (24.16) to recognition (24.31). We first examine this text from the perspective of the story audience.

The Emmaus scene addresses the disciples' blindness to Jesus. How do Jesus' students fail to recognize him after the resurrection? From a performance perspective, the Emmaus scene employs two neglected aspects of ancient rhetoric that would have been significant to a story audience as they understood the change in Jesus and the main characters: visualization and memory. As we discovered in the chapter on rhetoric, visualization and memory work well together to raise the listener to sublime contact with deity. In performance, an orator helps the audience visualize a scene through *ekphrasis*, "bringing what is portrayed clearly before the sight" (Theon *Progymnasmata* 118 [Kennedy, 45]). When speaking, the orator would "bring it before the eyes of [the] listeners" (Longinus *[Subl.]* (15.8). In rhetoric, visualization produces *enargeia* or vividness. Both produce emotion (*pathos*) and excitement (*kinesis*)[70] in the performer as well as the listener. In this scene, God comes to interact with them.

69. Nolland, *Luke,* 201.
70. Webb, "Imagination," 118.

Visualization is especially helpful for people whose physical condition (Quintilian *Inst.* 11.2.2) or fatigue (11.2.43) results in a struggle to recall sections of a speech. Much like *Ad herrenium,* Quintilian recommends visualizing symbols as an anchor for a house, a long journey, or buildings (11.2.20). This technique will improve those who are slow of heart and have difficulty recalling words they have been committed to memory (11.2.4) but who are trying to take the words to heart (11.2.29–35).

The Emmaus scene reflects visualization, recognition, memories, and divine contact. The passage uses visual language to describe their condition. They move from "their eyes were kept (held back)[71] from recognizing him" to "their eyes were opened." Retelling the story of Jesus of Nazareth, Cleopas describes vividly the tomb, the vision of angels, and the women. But these elements are not enough. The disciples need new memories and pictures of the experience to open their eyes. Recalling the events around Jesus or even the empty tomb and visions is not enough.

The disciples have two problems commonly associated with memory: forgetfulness and fatigue (Philo and Quintilian). Memory requires several stages of practice: information, recall, paraphrase, retention, forgetfulness, and repetition. The ultimate sign of a good memory is a changed life. The ideas are taken into the heart and affect the person's life going forward. The impressions are on the mind never to be forgotten.

In Luke, the disciples are "slow of heart," (24.25) a condition possibly brought on by their fatigue or grief over the loss of Jesus. We are not sure. The text does not tell us the cause of their problem, but the nature of memory in the ancient world indicates that this kind of condition is not a result of divine blinding.[72] At a narrative level, we might consider this issue to be one of being reluctant to believe.[73] From the perspective of performance, however, their teacher is training their memories. They are going through the process of learning how to recall words that are in their minds.[74] The only enemy of the community's memory is forgetfulness caused by failing to practice recollection. Not everyone learns

---

71. BADG, 448, s.v. "κρατέω."

72. Some commentators say that God prevented the disciples from understanding. Vinson, *Luke,* 750; I Marshall, *Luke,* 893; and Bock, *Luke,* 2:1911–1912.

73. Johnson, *Luke,* 395.

74. Marshall, 893, says the blindness enabled them to be prepared for a "fresh understanding" of prophecies of his resurrection.

or remembers at the same pace. Some memories and hearts are simply slower than others (Quint. *Inst.* 11.2.4; 11.2.29–35).

The teacher catches them from behind by surprise, listens to their dialogue, and challenges their memories of the story. They recognize Jesus not only by the visual clue of the bread, but also his interpretation of Moses, the prophets, and the scriptures in light of himself. In this context, memory is connected with belief. When they can recall the stories and the scriptures, they are led to believe.

As we have seen before in ancient storytelling, one version of the story is not always accepted in the conversation (Apuleius *Metam.* 1.20–21). Jesus corrects Cleopas's version of the events with strong emotion.[75] Jesus responds much like the storyteller in the scene from Apuleius correcting their retelling of the story. He reinterprets their memories around Moses and the prophets and uses the table and bread visually.

At this point, Luke writes, "Their eyes were opened," (24.31) a phrase unique in the New Testament.[76] What opens the eyes of the listeners? If God closed their eyes, then God presumably opens them.[77] Once again, the verb is passive; and the agent is not mentioned. The example from Luke, however, in light of performance suggests that the entire process of performance, visually and verbally, opens their eyes. The disciples' memories are reframed visually around the road, table, and bread. Their memories are changed with recollection about Moses and the prophets and new interpretations that form new impressions on their hearts.

If this is how the story audience responds, we can expect similar responses from the performance audience. The concealed hero in Greek drama is a familiar pattern to audiences of poetry (Homer *Odyssey* 16.160–189; 19.479–481). Revealing that which was concealed plays well in performing poetry (Aristotle *Poetics* 11.20–30; 17.15–20).[78] The performance audience visualizes the journey and a conversation among two friends and a stranger. They are enslaved to Jesus' story much like the emperor is to Aristides.

The responses of the story audience reflect what we would expect from a performance audience. In performance, the reader first visualizes

---

75. Marshall, *Luke*, 896; Bock, *Luke*, 2:1915.

76. Bock, *Luke*, 2:1918.

77. Marshall, *Luke*, 898.

78. Vinson, *Luke*, 747.

the scene in his mind so that he can help the listener picture the moment as well. When the orator places the visual element "before the listeners' eyes," they are energized. As Qunitilian says, the reader "makes us seem not so much to narrate as to exhibit the actual scene, while our emotions will be no less actively stirred than if we were present at the actual occurrence." (*Inst.* 6.2.29–32; Aristotle *Rhet.* 3.11.1411b.20). This is especially the case when we "set our souls on fire" when both orator and the listener feel the same as if we have "stood in their shoes" (*Inst.* 6.2.34–35). When this emotional response happens, the process of visualization with emotion takes the audience to transcendent submission. The performance enslaves the audience, moving them toward sublime contact with the divine (Longinus [*Subl.*] 15.9; *Inst.* 8.3.62, 67).[79] Around tables, visualizing this journey, they are able to retell the events of Jesus' life, teach one another how to rekindle memories, and take matters to heart. They retell the events to those in Jerusalem and reiterate the visual elements of the breaking of the bread (24.35).

In performance, the burning heart (singular) of the disciples, reframes the memories of Jesus and his disciples and uses visualization, memory, and emotion to achieve a different kind of effect. This event creates for the audience an identity with the disciples and Jesus, opens eyes that were held back from recognition, and demonstrates how the bread and table function within the life of the community.[80] The lector reflects the words of the teacher. He trains the performance audience how to use their memories in *paideia*. They go through a process, much like the story audience, of learning how to recall words and events of Jesus. Some are slower than others. They learn how to reinterpret prophecies from the Hebrew scriptures in light of the resurrection. They recognize Jesus in performance.

What emerges from the scene is one way at least the performance audience relates to Jesus' resurrection and participates with it. This pattern reflects the early church, but certain elements of this story reflect the performance. Memory links past, present, and future through visualizing the journey on the road from grief to community and from loss to resurrection. They imagine the scriptures that Jesus read.[81] The scene

79. Longinus, [*Subl.*]. 15.9 (Arieti and Crossett, Texts and Studies in Religion), 95.

80. Culpepper, "Luke," 480.

81. Vinson, *Luke,* 250.

from Emmaus, from the vantage point of performance, reflects a process of training the community how to remember, much like the book of Hebrews. Using the visual map of the Emmaus experience, the scene suggests that the table functions as a "site of memory." Jesus meets them on the road to practice recall, retelling, correcting, responding, *testimonia*, and eating. They experience sublime contact with God and each other because God comes to them. These disciples share an identity around the person. Their questions are received as part of the process of recognition and formation. The process functions as a way to keep their eyes open and their community together identified around the central figure of Jesus.

JESUS IN PERFORMANCE

Just as the New Testament refers to Jesus with many titles, so the performer of the Gospels and the audience listening have many descriptions of Jesus at their disposal. No one historical portrayal of Jesus stands out. In various ways and various places, they see him as prophet, storyteller, sage, humorist, riddler, and teacher. The performer's role is not to define Jesus but to enlarge the listener's soul. The receptive audience responds through these readings, sees each other in the mirror, and joined together in community listening.

In performance the canonical form of the Gospels is not the end but the beginning of the ways reader and audience interact. The story audience suggests a variety of ways that people responded to Jesus in performance, and the performance audience is just as multi-faceted. Performance criticism using ancient rhetorical conventions suggests that the performer and the audience work together collaboratively and elaborate on the script. These performances are emotional events that evoke a response from the audience and change with the reactions to the reader. The reader prepares for the performance of Jesus by paying attention to the rhetorical figures, gestures, and emotions in the text. The audience comes prepared to react and respond.

They read, correct, train, and teach each other. By doing so, they learn, recall, retain, and repeat the stories in a process of memory. They teach other an identity around the person of Jesus and the community with whom they listen. Some are slower than others, but all are part of a process of moving from information to recognition, from listening to interpretation.

The performances function as sites of memory for communities beginning to shape their identity. Many of the performances are connected visually around a table. The readings usually involve a table or are reminiscent of the table fellowship among Jesus and followers. The characterizations in performance function as the commemorative monuments to faithful living. The performance audience is linked to lists of people in genealogies who are now part of a list of faithful figures connected to the community. They are connected virtuously to others who are blessed by Jesus and whose character is being shaped in performance. The places remembered are repeated, retold, and relived through performance. In the process, they receive new memories to retell in performance. They continue the process of delivering the message of the gospel from memory and using the memories of previous performances.

5

Interpreting in Performance

THE NEW TESTAMENT INTERPRETER decides the value of a performance in the act of reading. When most people have been trained to read silently, disconnected from a community, the ancient performance never surfaces in discussion or study. Most interpreters dive into the questions of setting, date, authorship, and other historical matters without completing the process that the text in its canonical form suggests. The text is delivered to an audience.

A performance critical reading, however, argues that performance is a starting place for these historical-critical questions. We can begin from the performance in its final form and work outward. Here, the author's role behind the scenes of the writing of the text is minimal. The work is in the hands of the reader, with all the training and preparation that accompanies a person capable of delivering. The narrative is in a listener's ears, no longer distracted by what is happening but gazing on the performer and responding even before the reading begins.

Does applying this kind of analysis assist hermeneutics? Can we interpret a New Testament text in light of ancient performance? This book argues that by ignoring the oral performance, we have limited interpretation to meanings that come from silence and privacy. The ancient audience expands interpretation to public collaborative acts that invite audience and reader together into a working relationship of interpretation.

We have built on the work of others who have studied texts from folklore traditions,[1] modern media,[2] or dramatic reconstructions.[3] We have begun from the ancient concept of delivery and memory. Instead of ignoring the lector's and the audience's function, we are suggesting that the ancient rhetorical conventions of delivery and memory for performer and audience provide a way to reconstruct the performance imaginatively. For the story audience, we can understand some texts and responses more clearly. For the performance audience, we can suggest how they shape an early Christian *paideia*. Here we start from the Mediterranean world of *paideia* and suggest that their rhetorical conventions shape orators and audiences. By paying attention to ancient *paideia* we understand the value of performance to early Christian communities.

THE PERFORMER AS MIRROR

We have saved the most obvious yet the most difficult discussion for last: the *ethos* of the performer. As ancient rhetoric suggests, the performer's *ethos* affects the audience's interpretation the most. If the performer's character is questionable, the audience gives the performance little value. A trained orator is a model citizen and a good example for society. The speaker's *ethos* plays a significant role in persuasion, and to be a good orator requires being a "good man" (Quint. *Inst. Or.* 12.1.1–3; Plutarch [*Lib. ed*] 4 Mor. 2–3).

The early Christian communities defined *ethos* differently. People are no longer separated by good blood, wealth, or reputation. Instead, their conduct is shaped around the character of Jesus and the divine enablement and empowerment of the performer and community. Their *ethos* is shaped around his attributes and characteristics rather than simply the virtuous life of the Greco-Roman or Jewish society. The early Christian communities carve out a place for forgiveness in the midst of *ethos*. Conduct and the outcomes of a way of life matter. This conduct is enabled not by personal growth and fulfillment. Conduct is enabled in performance by divine empowerment and a community's instruction. To perform to a Christian community is to be instructed and vice-versa.

1. Thatcher, *Jesus the Riddler*, 39.
2. Boomershine, "Peter's Denial," 47–67
3. Swanson, *Provoking Matthew*, 118.

This study suggests that in a reading the performer becomes a mirror[4] of the virtues described in the text. Just as one holds up the lives of virtuous figures in the ancient world or views Jesus and gazes upon him, the reader reflects a pattern to the Christian community. This concept poses a significant challenge for reading simply for pleasure or for study separate from the effect. A person cannot read with the ancient audience in mind without an understanding of *ethos* and community. To read in light of ancient performance means by implication, one must assume some effect on the reader and community. By the time these texts are collected, they simply do not have a role apart from their circulation within the communities who are shaped together. From the ancient world's perspective, the performer is a part of the community, and the performer's life is a critical reflection of the process.

Interpretation in light of ancient performance shapes the reader in ways that other methods do not. The interpreter becomes a reader, and the reader needs a community. The community listens to the reader and follows because the community trusts the *ethos* of the interpreter. Reading, performance, response, and ethics come together for an interpreter wanting to engage the ancient world.

THE PERFORMANCE AUDIENCE AS CHILDREN

Several words describe what an audience does in the ancient world: "fellow-worker"[5] participant,[6] and listener; but in early Christian performance, the audience is being taught as children shaped around the character of the parent who instructs (*paideia*), educates, and disciplines as a loving father would his children. They are inquiring, questioning, and correcting participants in a process that allows them to form memories. They are adopted into a new community with brothers and sisters who are being parented around a new pattern. Reoriented, they address their God as "Our Father," see his son as a model of emulation, and begin to reframe their memories around this person.

---

4. David Rhoads suggests the performer is a medium or an artist. Here I am choosing to use the language of the ancient world to keep our footing there as a starting place for interpretation. Rhoads, *Reading Mark,* 182; and Rhoads, "Performance as Research," 170.

5. Maxwell, *Hearing Between the Lines,* 3.

6. Rhoads, *Reading Mark,* 171.

They collaborate, participate, remember, and digest the information. Here the definition of memory reflects an ancient understanding of the concept. Memory is more than past events or the recovery of sites where people erect monuments. Memory is not memorized texts retained in isolation by the select few who can remember verbatim. The ancient view of memory as a process is the key to understanding how an audience interprets a performance. When viewed from the perspective of the early Christian world, memory has a significant hermeneutical function. During a performance, the writer remembers texts, and the audience remembers characters and events differently. Through *testimonia,* and characterizations, they fill their minds with new information.

The early Christian audiences view memory as one way God touches the individual. The effect is different than the ancient world. As opposed to an elite group with certain powers of memories or men capable of being trained to have good memories, the memory of the individual and the group works collaboratively "wherever two or three were gathered" in Jesus' name (Matt 18.20).

The early believers do not separate soul from body as the Platonists did; instead, they see, much like their Jewish counterparts, the soul and body united. As the mind is affected by new information, the body is being transformed through character and habit formation.

These habits link them through a chain link of virtues using *sorites* with each other as part of the formation of the community and the people who are their fellow workers.

An example of how memory affects interpretation can be found in Stephen's paraphrase of Israel's history. As Mike Parsons shows, Stephen uses the conventions of ancient paraphrase as the story audience expects. When he speaks to the Sanhedrin, his paraphrase of Hebrew history enrages the crowd and makes them more motivated to execute him. In the performance of the text to an early Christian audience, however, Stephen probably becomes a role model for imitation or at least an example of how paraphrase could be used in performance. In the performance, the listeners remember not only Stephen but also his memory of Israel's history and his performance of that history.

Here memory does not contribute one meaning to the text any more than language does. Depending on the context, the listeners, the performer, and the setting, multiple meanings just as multiple memories were at work. We can say that the Gospel biographies of Jesus exemplify collections of multiple memories and perform differently even after they reach their final form. The importance for us here is that as they are delivered, all of these memories come alive in performance and have several effects on shaping the early Christian auditor.

Just as we see with the storytellers in Ovid, the audience responds (Ovid *Metam.* 9.325–392; 4.273). In this case, their memories are being informed with new or updated information. They are remembering Jesus and their own lives. They are viewing their lives as part of the earliest auditors of the voice from the "sacred mountain" (2 Peter 1). They are retelling stories to one another in the process of memory, and their conversations are the beginning of an emerging identity together as followers on the Way. Instead of viewing themselves as followers of a philosopher who draws students by magnetism, their performances empower them to retell what they hear. Whether they agreed with the performance or not is immaterial. Their conversations, debates, and decisions became a site of memory and the formation of a collective memory.

PERFORMING AND RESPONDING WITH THE ANCIENT AUDIENCE

We choose which audience with whom we perform every time we read early Christian texts. This book suggests, much like Markus Bockmuehl, that the earliest audiences have something to say about performance shaping virtuous communities. Christian performances are about not only a saving event but also a saving person who said, "This do in remembrance of me." As the texts are performed, they are remembering the person and the people who have become part of the living conversation within the performance.[7]

If we are going to dramatize the text around social and historical issues[8] or consider the folklore traditions of storytelling[9] or reconstruct the traditions of memory behind the performances,[10] then I am proposing that we consider these performances as they emerge during the first three

7. Bockmuehl, "New Testament Memory," in Barton, Stuckenbruck, and Wold, *Memory in the Bible,* 346, 356.

8. Swanson, *Provoking Mark,* 194–97.

9. Thatcher, *Jesus the Riddler,* 39.

10. Allison, *Constructing Jesus,* 17–20; and Bauckham, *Jesus and the Eyewitnesses,* 264–89.

centuries in the forms they are read and performed today. They provide for both performer and audience a script that begins with a different set of questions.

These performances, however, are not static events. Instead, the ancient world of performance encourages recall, retelling, paraphrase, and other forms of adaptation to the audience. The process is the act of memory that serves as a buffer against forgetfulness.

The Performer

Ancient performance conventions suggest that prior to reading the performer should give attention to the following:

1.   Note the emotions used by the performers in the story and the reactions in the story audience. Consider how to portray these characters. Choose tone of voice, intensity, and note how these change with repetition. Consider the emotions of pity, indignation, envy, and zeal as they reveal the character of the performer and audience. The performer considers if the story audience is a group to be emulated or rejected and reflects these reactions in reading. In a dialogue, choose how to characterize the dialogue between two characters. Adjust the face and the body to mark different characters, and vary the voice to indicate which character speaks.

2.   Choose how to remember the text. Because memory is not limited to rote memorization, the entire process of ancient memory can be utilized. The reader then chooses how to retain the text and elaborate within the performance. The process of memorization includes gathering information, taking notes on the arrangement of the text, deciding how to arrange the parts, planning where to digress, practicing the delivery, paraphrasing certain sections, and delivering the performance. Prepare for the delivery by creating mental images to store information. As the performer reads, the characters and locations fall into place to guide the performance. In a recitation, the performer can hold notes and choose when to elaborate, paraphrase and adapt to the audience. The performer is not limited to one version of the story and can vary from multiple translations as needed. The performer anticipates that during the reading, she will remember other

stories and *testimonia* that fit the recitation.

3. Choose which gestures to imitate and how they will be performed. Ancient gestures do not match cultural conventions today. For instance, the gesture for silence in the ancient world is likely and upraised fifth finger. Today, the sign for quiet is the index finger over the lips. The performer decides bodily movement, whether to sit or stand, to run, or to move around the room. Consider if people will be called out of the audience. Place objects around the room to use as visual clues to the audience and performer.

4. Mark and signal different parts of the speech. Quintilian indicates that parts of a speech should be marked nonverbally. The analysis of the rhetorical components of a work signals the emotional significance of the section to the orator. The performer indicates these through gestures and changes in intensity. As Ron Allen suggests, location on the stage can also mark different sections of a speech.

5. The performer's *ethos* will be confirmed or questioned in light of the performance. The performer holds a mirror between text and audience for the audience to reflect upon their condition. The performer should pay attention to her own character and reflection of the virtues in the text. In a Christian community, the act of performance is *paideia* of the performer. To train for performance is to train one's character. If one's behavior does not match the characters in performance, an audience may not respond to what they see. The performer may also use the performance as a way to enlarge her character. The performer changes as a result of the delivery.

6. The performer needs to speak to the audience ahead of time, previewing what will be said so the audience can participate more fully. (Aristotle *Rhet.* 3.16.1417b). If the audience becomes disengaged, the performer may need to recapture their attention with a digression or an aside. Note when the text uses audience inclusion and crosses the boundaries between story and performance audience with such phrases, "Whoever has ears to hear," and "Listen!" Plan to use a gaze and gesture to invite the audience to participate. Remain silent in places where the audience needs

to fill in the gaps of an open-ended story or enthymeme.

The Audience

The listeners have a part to play much like the performer. They play the role of the performance audience and pay attention to the performer as if she is a mirror causing them to reflect on their condition. Ancient conventions suggest the listener comes prepared to interrupt, debate, converse, and respond.

1. The performance changes and affects the memory of the auditor. As the text is performed, the audience remembers stories and images. The audience takes notes and compares the pictures in performance with the picture in his mind.

2. The audience responds when appropriate, and most of the time, any time is appropriate. The audience reacts to the story by taking notes, retelling, and remembering, The audience responds to the performance with preparation, applause, interruptions, questions, and challenges.

3. The audience gazes into the mirror of the performer and reflects on their condition. The audience sees responds emotionally and virtuously to the character of Jesus and the community around Jesus. They are taken to a moment of sublime, divine intervention in their lives where their souls are enlarged and expanded because of the performance.

4. The performance links individual to each other in community. As students and listeners, they are reflected together in performance and are part of a community of listeners. They are given roles to carry out together with a new identity shaped by the performance.

5. The listeners disagree and respond to one another. The audience chooses how to correct the performer and to correct each other. The audience gives feedback to one another and tells other stories to each other that amplify the performance. They become a part of the process of memory.

6. Following the performance, the audience continues the conversation. They talk to each other; they retell the message; they return to hear more.

7. The performance becomes an act of *paideia*. The community is formed culturally around the person of Jesus. They learn about discipline, suffering, and difficulties. They reflect on their condition and learn the parental role of God through the performance.

8. The audience receives grace in performance. Because the act of performance is a part of the contact with the divine, the performance is an act of grace that teaches and trains the listener. This grace trains and educates the listener in an identity formed around Jesus.

These performances resist the tendency to isolate phrases or individual verses from the New Testament or ignore the emotive value of the texts. A virtuous community uses Jesus' *logia*, maxims, and *chreia* as part of a larger performer's world. Even Paul's statement "It is better to give than receive" fit an appeal to remember and respond. Preparation and performance should not isolate phrases or verses from the Bible but instead should fit the performance of a larger narrative that includes questions, challenges, interrogations, and response. Within the performance are conflict, disagreement, and, in the process, formation.

By performing with the ancient audiences, we shape *paideia*, whether in classroom or the congregation. If a community wants to shape the character of their members, or a teacher her students, they assign one person to become the lector. The practice is an act of character formation. The ethos of the reader is shaped; and based on ancient practices of *paideia*, the life of the reader is changed virtuously to reflect the figures in the text. The audience trains one another in forming their opinions, correcting one another, and living out these claims together.

We now have another layer of interpretation that we can add. When performing, we not only take into account the performer and the audience, but also bring a whole new set of questions and possibilities for interpretation. What could the audience have remembered? How were stories being reshaped in the telling? How did vocal inflection and gestures affect their memory of events?

We can certainly, as Richard Swanson has done, set the performance's context, discussing the political and social realities of the day. Much work has been done in this area; and we should be grateful for it. It seems unclear to me, however, how these political and social forces would bring to bear on the performance of the text itself. We cannot say much about

Herod unless Herod of course is being performed. We can note, however, the social dynamics of the day but give particular attention to how the performance of these stories affected their memories of other things and people that were part of the ongoing narrative and dialogue within the world of rhetoric. That is, the rhetorical, philosophical, and storytelling schools have much to say about the effect of memory and what if anything audiences remembered. This becomes a part of a larger discussion of the rhetorical effect that the delivery has on the audience. We would not want to overlook the historical and political issues surrounding the first century. But we also would not want to omit the very significant rhetorical effect happening in the audience that would be a part of the natural expectations of people who regularly saw and heard performances in their society, in the agora, or as part of a synagogue performance.

For instance, in one sense we could view Matthew's prologue as a recollection of memories, a reframing of the genealogy of Jesus. The performance of these names has a certain impact on the audience. The genealogy includes names in patterns of twelve and individuals with dubious backgrounds. In light of the "outcome" of the faith in Hebrews, Matthew's history of Jesus family is viewed as instruction and *paideia* about the outcome of the lives of these figures. Just as in a performance of Homer, the list "warms up" the audience, so in Matthew the genealogy is read with a sense of anticipation. The performer's audience responds with a sense of anticipation energized by what they were hearing, and remembering names differently. The legacy of those who were once considered sinners are now preview the beginning of a new royal line.

Reading with the ancient audience requires a different kind of work for both reader and listener. The performer gives attention to his or her *ethos* as a reader to the community. Before reading, the performer takes into account the rhetorical structure of the text and the ways the emotions and gestures can be performed. The performer is first part of the audience, learning to read, listen, respond, and change.

The audience comes prepared to play a part. They interrupt, applaud, suggest, respond, and correct the performer and each other. They fill in the gaps and evaluate the performance through their behavior, both in the reading and in the living. The emotional nature of texts connects to character formation. In ancient performance, the interpreter cannot remain disengaged or disconnected with the characters as remote figures from afar. Instead, they become a part of the "living voice" of performance that was once heard on the sacred mountain and has been retold from memory for generations. They continue to deliver from memory.

Bibliography

Achtemeier, Paul J. "Omne Verbum Sonat: The New Testament and the Oral Environment of Late Western Antiquity." *Journal of Biblical Literature* 109 (1990) 3–27.

Aelius Theon et. al. *Progymnasmata: Greek Textbooks of Prose Composition and Rhetoric.* In vol. 10 of *Writings from the Greco Roman World.* Translated by George A. Kennedy. Atlanta: Society of Biblical Literature, 2003.

Alexandre, Manuel. "Rhetorical Argumentation as an Exegetical Technique in Philo of Alexandria." In *Hellenica et Judaica: hommage à Valentin Nikiprowetzky,* edited by André Caquot, Mireille Hadas-Lebel, and J. Riaud, 13–27. Leuven: Peeters, 1986.

Allen, Ronald J. "Performance and the New Testament in Preaching." In *Performance in Preaching: Bringing the Sermon to Life,* edited by Jana Childers and Clayton J. Schmit, 99–116. Engaging Worship. Grand Rapids: Baker Academic, 2008.

Allison, Dale C. *Constructing Jesus: Memory, Imagination, and History.* Grand Rapids: Baker Academic, 2010.

Anderson, Graham. *The Second Sophistic: A Cultural Phenomenon in the Roman Empire.* New York: Routledge, 1993.

Apuleius. *Metamorphoses.* Edited and translated by J. Arthur Hanson. 2 vols. LCL 1. Cambridge, MA: Harvard University Press, 1989.

Aristides, P. Aelius. *Orations XVII-LIII.* Translated by Charles A. Behr. Vol. 2 of *The Complete Works.* Leiden: Brill, 1981.

Aristotle. *Oeconomica.* Edited by T. E. Page. Translated by G. Cyril Armstrong. 2 vols. LCL 2. Cambridge, MA: Harvard University Press, 1958.

———. *On Rhetoric: a Theory of Civic Discourse.* Translated by George A. Kennedy. 2. New York: Oxford University Press, 2007.

Arrian. *Epictetus: The Discourses as Reported by Arrian, the Manual, and Fragments.* Translated by W. A. Oldfather. 2 vols. LCL. Cambridge, MA: Harvard University Press, 1959.

Balogh, E. "Voces Paginarum: Beiträge zur Geschichte des lauten Lesens und Schreibens." *Philologus* 82 (1926–1927) 84–109.

Barton, Stephen C. "Memory and Remembrance in Paul." In *Memory in the Bible and Antiquity: the Fifth Durham-Tübingen Research Symposium,* edited by Stephen C. Barton, Loren T. Stuckenbruck, and Benjamin G. Wold, 321–40. Wissenschaftliche Untersuchungen zum Neuen Testament 212. Tübingen: Mohr Siebeck, 2007.

Barton, Stephen C., Loren T. Stuckenbruck, and Benjamin G. Wold, editors. *Memory in the Bible and Antiquity: the Fifth Durham-Tübingen Research Symposium.*

Wissenschaftliche Untersuchungen zum Neuen Testament 212. Tübingen: Mohr Siebeck, 2007.

Bauckham, Richard J. *Jesus and the Eyewitnesses: the Gospels as Eyewitness Testimony.* Grand Rapids: Eerdmans, 2006.

———. *Jude, 2 Peter.* Word Biblical Commentary 50. Waco: Word, 1983.

Bauer, W., F.W. Danker, W.F. Arndt, and F.W. Gingrich, editors. *Greek-English Lexicon of the New Testament and other Early Christian Literature.* 3. Chicago: University of Chicago Press, 1999.

Beavis, Mary Ann. *Mark's Audience: The Literary and Social Setting of Mark 4.11-12.* Journal for the Study of the New Testament Supplement Series 33. Sheffield: Sheffield Academic, 1989.

Blomberg, Craig L. *Interpreting the Parables.* Downers Grove: InterVarsity, 1990.

Bloomquist, L. Gregory. "Subverted by Joy: Suffering and Joy in Paul's Letter to the Philippians." *Interpretation* 61 (2007) 270–82.

Bock, Darrell L. *Luke.* 2 vols. Baker Exegetical Commentary on the New Testament 2. Grand Rapids: Baker Books, 1996.

Bockmuehl, Markus. "New Testament Wirkungsgeschichte and the Early Christian Appeal to Living Memory." In *Memory in the Bible and Antiquity: the Fifth Durham-Tübingen Research Symposium,* edited by Stephen C. Barton, Loren T. Stuckenbruck, and Benjamin G. Wold, 341–68. Wissenschaftliche Untersuchungen zum Neuen Testament 212. Tübingen: Mohr Siebeck, 2007.

———. *Seeing the Word: Refocusing New Testament Study.* Grand Rapids: Baker Academic, 2006.

Boegehold, Alan L. *When a Gesture was Expected: a Selection of Examples from Archaic and Classical Greek Literature.* Princeton: Princeton University Press, 1999.

Boring, M. Eugene. "Matthew." In vol. 8 of *The New Interpreter's Bible,* edited by Leander Keck, 87–506. Nashville: Abingdon, 1987.

Botha, Pieter J. J. "The Verbal Art of the Pauline Letters: Rhetoric, Performance and Presence." In *Rhetoric and the New Testament: Essays from the 1992 Heidelberg Conference,* edited by Stanley E. Porter and Thomas Olbricht, 409–428. Journal for the Study of the New Testament Supplement Series 90. Sheffield: Sheffield Academic, 1993.

Bradley, K. R. *Slaves and Masters in the Roman Empire: a Study in Social Control.* Collection Latomus 185. Bruxelles: Latomus, 1984.

Bradley, Keith. *Slavery and Society at Rome.* Key Themes in Ancient History. Cambridge: Cambridge University Press, 1994.

Braund, Susanna Morton, and Christopher Gill, editors. *The Passions in Roman Thought and Literature.* Cambridge: Cambridge University Press, 1997.

Brisson, E. Carson. "Matthew 25:14–30." *Interpretation* 56 (2002) 207–10.

Buitenwerf, Rieuwerd, Harm W. Hollander, and Johannes Tromp, editors. *Jesus, Paul, and Early Christianity: Studies in Honour of Henk Jan de Jonge.* Novum Testamentum Supplements 130. Leiden: Brill, 2008.

Caquot, André, Mireille Hadas-Lebel, and J. Riaud, editors. *Hellenica et Judaica: hommage à Valentin Nikiprowetzky.* Leuven: Peeters, 1986.

Carr, David M. *Writing on the Tablet of the Heart.* Writing on the Heart. Oxford: Oxford University Press, 2005.

Carter, Warren, and John Paul Heil. *Matthew's Parables: Audience-oriented Perspectives.* Catholic Biblical Quarterly Monograph Series 30. Washington, D.C.: Catholic Biblical Assciation of America, 1998.

Cato, Marcus Porcius. *On Agriculture.* Translated by William Davis Hooper. LCL. Cambridge, MA: Harvard University Press, 1954.

Charlesworth, James H. *The Old Testament Pseudepigrapha.* 2 vols. Anchor Bible Reference Library. New York: Doubleday, 1983.

Childers, Jana, and Clayton J. Schmit, editors. *Performance in Preaching: Bringing the Sermon to Life.* Engaging Worship. Baker Academic: Grand Rapids, 2008.

Cicero, Marcus Tullius. *Brutus Orator.* Translated by H. M. Hubbell. LCL. Cambridge, MA: Harvard University Press, 1942.

———. *De Oratore.* Translated by E. W. Sutton. LCL. Cambridge, MA: Harvard University Press, 1979.

———. *Pro Sexto Roscio Amerino.* Edited by T. E. Page. Translated by John Henry Freese. LCL. Cambridge, MA: Harvard University Press, 1956.

———. *Tusculan Disputations.* Translated by A. E. Douglas. 2 vols. Chicago: Bolchazy-Carducci, 1985.

Culpepper, R. Alan. *Mark.* Smyth & Helwys Bible Commentary. Macon: Smyth and Helwys, 2007.

Davids, Peter H. *The Letters of 2 Peter and Jude.* Pillar New Testament Commentary. Grand Rapids: Eerdmans, 2006.

Davies, William David, and Dale C. Allison. *A Critical and Exegetical Commentary on the Gospel According to Matthew.* 3 vols. International Critical Commentary. Edinburgh: T&T Clark, 1997.

Derrett, J. Duncan M. *Law in the New Testament.* London: Darton, Longman, and Todd, 1970.

Dibelius, Martin and Hans Conzelmann. *The Pastoral Epistles: a Commentary on the Pastoral Epistles.* Hermeneia. Minneapolis: Fortress, 1972.

Dionysius of Halicarnassus. *The Roman Antiquities.* Edited by T. E. Page. Translated by Earnest Cary. 7 vols. LCL 2. Cambridge, MA: Harvard University Press, 1937.

Dominik, William J., editor. *Roman Eloquence: Rhetoric in Society and Literature.* New York: Routledge, 1997.

Dunn, James D. G. *Jesus Remembered.* Christianity in the Making 1. Grand Rapids: Eerdmans, 2003.

Fitzgerald, John T., Dirk Obbink, and Glenn S. Holland, editors. *Philodemus and the New Testament World.* Supplements to Novum Testamentum 111. Boston: Brill, 2004.

Fitzgerald, John T., editor. *Passions and Moral Progress in Greco-Roman Thought.* New York: Routledge, 2008.

Flavius Josephus. *Life of Josephus.* In vol. 9 of *Flavius Josephus: Translation and Commentary.* Edited and translated by Steve Mason. Boston: Brill, 2001.

France, R. T. *The Gospel of Mark: A Commentary on the Greek Text.* New International Greek Testament Commentary. Grand Rapids: Eerdmans, 2002.

Fronto, Marcus Cornelius. Translated by C. R. Haines. 2 vols. LCL. Cambridge, MA: Harvard University Press: 1962.

Gavrilov, A. K. "Techniques of Reading in Classical Antiquity." *Classical Quarterly* 47 (1997) 56–73.

Garland, David E. *Mark.* The NIV Application Commentary. Grand Rapids: Zondervan, 1996.

————. *Reading Matthew: A Literary and Theological Commentary on the First Gospel.* Edited by Charles H. Talbert. Reading the New Testament Series 1. New York: Crossroad, 1995.

Gloer, Hulitt. *1 & 2 Timothy-Titus.* Smyth & Helwys Bible Commentary. Macon: Smyth & Helwys, 2010.

Grimaldi, William M. A. *Aristotle, Rhetoric II: A Commentary.* New York: Fordham University Press, 1988.

Gruen, Erich S. *Heritage and Hellenism: the Reinvention of Jewish Tradition.* Hellenistic Culture and Society 30. Berkeley: University of California Press, 1998.

Guelich, Robert A. *Mark 1—8:26.* Edited by Ralph P. Martin. Word Biblical Commentary 34a. Dallas: Word, 1989.

Hadot, Pierre. *What is Ancient Philosophy.* Translated by Michael Chase. Cambridge: Belknap, 2002.

Haenchen, Ernst. *The Acts of the Apostles: a Commentary.* Basil Blackwell: Oxford, 1971.

Hagner, Donald A. *Matthew 14–28.* Edited by Ralph P. Martin. Word Biblical Commentary 33b. Dallas: Word, 1995.

Hauerwas, Stanley. *Matthew.* Edited by R. R. Reno. Brazos Theological Commentary on the Bible. Grand Rapids: Brazos, 2006.

Hearon, Holly E. "Storytelling in Oral and Written Media Contexts of the Ancient Mediterranean World." In *Jesus, the Voice, and the Text: Beyond the Oral and the Written Gospel,* edited by Tom Thatcher, 89–110. Waco: Baylor University Press, 2008.

————. *The Mary Magdalene Tradition: Witness and Counter-Witness in Early Christian Communities.* Collegeville, MN: Liturgical, 2004.

Hearon, Holly E., and Philip Ruge-Jones, editors. *The Bible in Ancient and Modern Media: Essays in Honor of Tom Boomershine.* Biblical Performance Criticism: Orality, Memory, Translation, Rhetoric, Discourse. Eugene, OR: Cascade, 2009.

Hippolytus of Rome. *The Apostolic Tradition of Hippolytus.* Translated by Burton Scott Eason. New York: MacMillan, 1934.

————. *The Liturgy of the Eighth Book of 'The Apostolic Constitutions' Commonly Called The Clementine Liturgy.* Translated by R. H. Cresswell. New York: MacMillan, 1924.

————. *The Treatise on the Apostolic Tradition.* Edited by Gregory Dix. London: SPCK: 1968.

Horbury, William. "The Remembrance of God in the Psalms of Solomon." In *Memory in the Bible and Antiquity: the Fifth Durham-Tübingen Research Symposium,* edited by Stephen C. Barton, Loren T. Stuckenbruck, and Benjamin G. Wold, 111–28. Wissenschaftliche Untersuchungen zum Neuen Testament 212. Tübingen: Mohr Siebeck, 2007.

Jaeger, Werner. *Early Christianity and Greek Paideia.* Cambridge: Belknap, 1961.

Jeremias, Joachim. *The Parables of Jesus.* Translated by S. H. Hooke 2. Gottingen: Vandenhoeck and Ruprecht, 1970. Repr., Upper Saddle River, New Jersey: Prentice Hall, 1972.

Johnson, Luke Timothy. *Hebrews: A Commentary.* The New Testament Library. Louisville: Westminster John Knox, 2006.

————. *Religious Experience in Earliest Christianity: a Missing Dimension in New Testament Studies.* Minneapolis: Fortress, 1998.

————. *The Acts of the Apostles.* Sacra Pagina 5. Collegeville, MN: Liturgical, 1992.

Johnson, William A. *Readers and Reading Culture in the High Roman Empire: a Study of Elite Communities*. Classical Culture and Society. Oxford: Oxford University Press, 2010.

———. "Oral performance and the Composition of Herodotus' Histories." *Greek, Roman and Byzantine Studies* 35 (Autumn 1994) 229–54.

———. "Toward a Sociology of Reading in Classical Antiquity." *AJP* 121 (2000) 593–627.

Josephus. Translated by H. St. J. Thackeray et al. 10 vols. LCL. Cambridge, MA: Harvard University Press, 1926–1965.

Keener, Craig S. *The Gospel of Matthew: A Socio-Rhetorical Commentary*. Grand Rapids: Eerdmans, 2009.

Kelly, H. A. "Tragedy and the Performance of Tragedy in Late Roman Antiquity." *Traditio* 35 (1979) 21–44.

Kennedy, George A. *The Art of Rhetoric in the Roman World 300 B. C.-A. D. 300*. Princeton: Princeton University Press, 1972.

———. *Greek Rhetoric Under Christian Emperors*. Princeton: Princeton University Press, 1983.

———. *A New History of Classical Rhetoric*. Princeton: Princeton University Press, 1994.

———. *New Testament Interpretation through Rhetorical Criticism*. Chapel Hill: University of North Carolina Press, 1984.

———, trans. *Progymnasmata: Greek Textbooks of Prose Composition and Rhetoric*. Writings from the Greco Roman World 10. Atlanta: Society of Biblical Literature, 2003.

Lane, William L. *Hebrews 9–13*. World Biblical Commentary 47b. Dallas: Word, 1991.

Levene, D. S. "Pity, Fear, and the Historical Audience: Tacitus on the fall of Vitellius." In *The Passions in Roman Thought and Literature,* edited by Susanna Morton Braund and Christopher Gill, 128–49. Cambridge: Cambridge University Press, 1997.

Longinus. *On the Sublime*. Translated by James A. Arieti and John M. Crossett. Texts and Studies in Religion 21. New York: Mellen, 1985.

Lucian. Translated by A. M. Harmon. 8 vols. LCL. Cambridge, MA: Harvard University Press, 1969.

Lysias. Translated by W. R. M. Lamb. LCL. Cambridge, MA: Harvard University Press, 1957.

Mack, Burton L. "Decoding the Scripture: Philo and the Rules of Rhetoric." In *Nourished with Peace: Studies in Hellenistic Judaism in Memory of Samuel Sandmel,* edited by Frederick E. Greenshpahn, Earle Hilgert, and Burton L. Mack, 81–115. Chico: Scholars, 1984.

Mack, Burton L., and Vernon K. Robbins. *Patterns of Persuasion in the Gospels*. Sonoma, CA: Polebridge, 1989.

Maier-Eichhorn, Ursula. *Die Gestikulation in Quintilians Rhetorik*. Europäsiche Hochschulschriften. Klassiche Sprachen und Literaturen, ser. 15, vol. 41. Frankfurt am Main: Peter Lang, 1989.

Marshall, I. Howard. *The Gospel of Luke: A Commentary on the Greek Text*. New International Greek Testament Commentary. Grand Rapids: Eerdmans, 1978.

Martial. *Epigrams*. Translated by David Roy Shackleton Bailey. 3 vols. LCL. Cambridge, MA: Harvard University Press, 1993.

Maxwell, Kathy Reiko. *Hearing Between the Lines: The Audience as Fellow-Worker in Luke-Acts and is Literary Milieu*. Library of New Testament Studies 425. New York: T. & T. Clark, 2010.

Mendels, Doron. *Memory in Jewish, Pagan, and Christian Societies of the Graeco-Roman World*. New York: T. & T. Clark, 2004.

———. "Societies of Memory in the Graeco-Roman World." In *Memory in the Bible and Antiquity: the Fifth Durham-Tübingen Research Symposium*, edited by Stephen C. Barton, Loren T. Stuckenbruck, and Benjamin G. Wold, 143–62. Wissenschaftliche Untersuchungen zum Neuen Testament 212. Tübingen: Mohr Siebeck, 2007.

Minchin, Elizabeth. "The Performance of Lists and Catalogues in the Homeric Epics." In *Voice into Text: Orality and Literacy in Ancient Greece*, edited by Ian Worthington, 3–20. Mnemosyne, Bibliotheca Classica Batava 157. New York: Brill, 1996.

Mittman-Reichert, Ulrike. "Erinerrung und Heilserkenntnis im Lukasevangelium: Ein Beitrag zum neutestamentalichen Verständnis des Abendmahls." In *Memory in the Bible and Antiquity*, edited by Loren T. Stuckenbruck, Stephen C. Barton, and Benjamin G. Wold, 243–73. Wissenschaftliche Untersuchungen zum Neuen Testament 212. Tübingen: Mohr Siebeck, 2007.

Niditch, Susan. *Oral World and Written Word*. Louisville: Westminster John Knox, 1991.

Noakes, Susan. "Gracious Words: Luke's Jesus and the Reading of Sacred Poetry at the Beginning of the Christian Era." In *The Ethnography of Reading*, edited by Jonathan Boyarin, 38–57. Berkeley: University of California Press, 1992.

Nolland, John. *The Gospel of Matthew: a Commentary on the Greek Text*. New International Greek Testament Commentary. Grand Rapids: Eerdmans, 2005.

Olbricht, Thomas H. "Delivery and Memory." In *Handbook of Classical Rhetoric in the Hellenistic Period: 330 B.C.-A.D. 400*, edited by Stanley E. Porter, 159–70. New York: Brill, 1997.

Ovid. *Metamorphoses*. Edited by G. P. Goold. Translated by Frank Justus Miller. 6 vols. LCL. Cambridge, MA: Harvard University Press, 1954.

Parsons, Mikeal C. *Acts*. Edited by Mikeal C. Parsons and Charles H. Talbert. Paideia Commentaries on the New Testament. Grand Rapids: Baker Academic, 2008.

Philo. Edited by T. E. Page. Translated by F.H. Colson and G.H. Whitaker. 11 vols. LCL. Cambridge, MA: Harvard University Press, 1949.

Philostratus. *Imagines*. Translated by Arthur Fairbanks. LCL. Cambridge, MA: Harvard University Press, 1960.

———. *Vitae sophistratarum*. Edited by Wilmer Cave France Wright. Translated by Wilmer Cave France Wright. LCL. Cambridge, MA: Harvard University Press, 1952.

Plato. Translated by H. N. Fowler. 10 vols. LCL. Cambridge, MA: Harvard University Press, 1967.

Pliny. *Letters*. Translated by William Melmoth. 2 vols. LCL. Cambridge, MA: Harvard University Press, 1940.

Polybius. *Historiae*. Translated by W. R. Paton. Cambridge, MA: Harvard University Press, 1972-1979.

Polycarp. *To the Philippians*. Translated by Kirsopp Lake. LCL. Cambridge, MA: Harvard University Press, 1985.

Porter, Stanley E., editor. *Handbook of Classical Rhetoric in the Hellenistic Period: 330 B.C.-A.D. 400*. New York: Brill, 1997.

Rhoads, David. "Biblical Performance Criticism: Performance as Research." *Oral Tradition* 25 (2010) 157–98. Online: http://journal.oraltradition.org/issues/25i/rhoads.

———. "Performance Criticism: an Emerging Methodology in Second Testament Studies." *Biblical Theology Bulletin* 36 (2006) 118–33.

————. "What is Performance Criticism." In *The Bible in Ancient and Modern Media: Essays in Honor of Tom Boomershine,* edited by Holly E. Hearon and Philip Ruge-Jones, 83–100. Biblical Performance Criticism: Orality, Memory, Translation, Rhetoric, Discourse. Eugene, OR: Cascade, 2009.

Richlin, Amy. "Gender and Rhetoric: Producing Manhood in the Schools." In *Roman Eloquence: Rhetoric in Society and Literature,* edited by William J. Dominik, 90-110. New York: Routledge, 1997.

Rimell, Victoria. *Martial's Rome: Empire and the Ideology of Epigram.* Cambridge: Cambridge University Press, 2008.

Rohrbaugh, Richard. "A Peasant Reading of the Parable of the Talents/Pounds: a Text of Terror." *Biblical Theology Bulletin* 23 (1993) 32–39.

Scott, Bernard Brandon. *Hear then the Parable: A Commentary on the Parables of Jesus.* Minneapolis: Fortress, 1989.

Seneca. *De Beneficiis.* Edited by T. E. Page. Translated by John W. Basore. 3 vols. LCL 3. 1935. Repr., Cambridge, MA: Harvard University Press, 1958.

————. *Ad Lucilium Epistulae Morales.* Translated by Richard M. Gummere. 3 vols. LCL. Cambridge, MA: Harvard University Press, 1970–1979.

Shepherd of Hermas. *Similitudes.* Translated by Kirsopp Lake. LCL. Cambridge, MA: Harvard University Press, 1985.

Shiell, William D. *Reading Acts: The Lector and the Early Christian Audience.* Edited by R. Alan Culpepper, Rolf Rendtorff, and Ellen Van Wolde. Biblical Interpretation 70. Boston: Brill, 2004.

Shillington, V. George, editor. *Jesus and His Parables: Interpreting the Parables of Jesus Today.* Edinburgh: T. & T. Clark, 1997.

Shiner, Whitney. *Proclaiming the Gospel: First-Century Performance of Mark.* New York: Trinity, 2003.

Small, Jocelyn Penny. *Wax Tablets of the Mind: Cognitive Studies of Memory and Literacy in Classical Antiquity.* New York: Routledge, 1997.

Smith, Dennis E., and Michael E. Williams, editors. *The Parables of Jesus.* Vol. 11 of *The Storyteller's Companion to the Bible.* Nashville: Abingdon, 2006.

Snodgrass, Klyne. *Stories with Intent: a Comprehensive Guide to the Parables of Jesus.* Grand Rapids: Eerdmans, 2008.

Soards, Marion L. *The Speeches in Acts: their Content, Context, and Concerns.* Louisville, KY: Westminster John Knox, 1994.

Sonkowsky, Robert P. "An Aspect of Delivery in Ancient Rhetorical Theory." *Transactions and Proceedings of the American Philological Association* 90 (1959) 256–74.

Sophocles. Translated by F. Storr. 2 vols. LCL. Cambridge, MA: Harvard University Press, 1977.

Stettler, Hanna. *Die Christologie der Pastoralbriefe.* Wissenschaftliche Untersuchungen zum Neuen Testament 195. Tübingen: Mohr Siebeck, 1998.

Stuckenbruck, Loren T., Stephen C. Barton, and Benjamin G. Wold, editors. *Memory in the Bible and Antiquity.* Wissenschaftliche Untersuchungen zum Neuen Testament 212. Tübingen: Mohr Siebeck, 2007.

Suetonius. Translated by John C. Rolfe. 2 vols. LCL. Cambridge, MA: Harvard University Press, 1979.

Suetonius. *De Gramaticis et Rhetoribus.* Translated by Robert A. Kaster. LCL. Cambridge, MA: Harvard University Press, 1995.

Swanson, Richard W. *Provoking the Gospel of Luke: a Storyteller's Commentary, Year C.* Cleveland: Pilgrim, 2006.

Tacitus. *Tacitus' Agricola, Germany, and Dialogue on Orators.* Translated by Herbert W. Benario. Norman: University of Oklahoma Press, 1991.

Talbert, Charles. *Learning through Suffering: The Educational Value of Suffering in the New Testament and in its Milieu.* Collegeville, Minnesota: Michael Glazier, 1991.

———. *Matthew.* Edited by Charles H. Talbert and Mikeal C. Parsons. Paideia Commentaries on the New Testament. Grand Rapids: Baker Academic, 2010.

———. *Reading the Sermon on the Mount: Character Formation and Decision Making in Matthew 5-7.* Columbia: University of South Carolina Press, 2004. Repr., Grand Rapids: Baker Academic, 2006.

Tannehill, Robert C. *The Acts of the Apostles.* Vol. 2 of *The Narrative Unity of Luke-Acts: a Literary Interpretation.* Minneapolis: Fortress, 1990.

Thatcher, Tom. *Jesus the Riddler: The Power of Ambiguity in the Gospels.* Louisville: Westminster John Knox, 2006.

———, editor. *Jesus, the Voice, and the Text: Beyond the Oral and the Written Gospel.* Waco: Baylor University Press, 2008.

The Apostolic Fathers. Translated by Kirsopp Lake. 2 vols. LCL. Cambridge, MA: Harvard University Press, 1985.

Theocritus. Translated by A. S. F. Gow. 2 vols. Cambridge: Cambridge University Press, 1992.

Thompson, James W. *Hebrews.* Paideia: Commentaies on the New Testament. Grand Rapids: Baker Academic, 2008.

Thucydides. Translated by Charles Forster Smith. 4 vols. LCL. Cambridge, MA: Harvard University Press, 1930.

Tilley, Maureen A., trans. *Donatist Martyr Stories: the Church in Conflict in Roman North Africa.* Translated Texts for Historians 24. Liverpool: Liverpool University Press, 1996.

Tolbert, Mary Ann. *Sowing the Gospel: Mark's World in Literary-Historical Perspective.* Minneapolis: Fortress, 1989.

Turner, David L. *Matthew.* Baker Exegetical Commentary on the New Testament. Grand Rapids: Baker Academic, 2008.

Valerius Maximus. *Memorable Doings and Sayings.* Translated by David Roy Bailey. 2 vols. LCL 2. Cambridge, MA: Harvard University Press, 2000.

Varro, Marcus Terrentius. *On Agriculture.* Translated by William Davis Hooper. LCL. Cambridge, MA: Harvard University Press, 1954.

Vinson, Richard B. *Luke.* Smyth & Helwys Bible Commentary. Macon: Smyth & Helwys, 2008.

Ward, Richard. "Pauline Voice and Presence as a Strategic Communication." *Semeia* 65 (1994) 95–107.

———. *Speaking of the Holy: the Art of Communication in Preaching.* St. Louis: Chalice, 2001.

Ware, James. "Moral Progress and Divine Power in Seneca and Paul." In *Passions and Moral Progress in Greco-Roman Thought,* edited by John T. Fitzgerald, 267–83. New York: Routledge, 2008.

Watson, Duane F. "Paul's Speech to the Ephesian Elders (Acts 20.17-38): Epideictic Rhetoric of Farewell." In *Persuasive Artistry: Studies in New Testament Rhetoric in Honor of George A. Kennedy,* edited by Duane F. Watson, 184–208. Journal for the

Study of the New Testament: Supplement Series 50. Sheffield: Sheffield Academic, 1991.

Watson, Duane F., and Hauser, Alan J. *Rhetorical Criticism of the Bible: a Comprehensive Bibliography with Notes on History and Method.* Leiden: Brill, 1994.

Webb, Ruth. "Imagination and the Arousal of Emotions in Greco-Roman Rhetoric." In *The Passions in Roman Thought and Literature,* edited by Susanna Morton Braund and Christopher Gill, 112–27. Cambridge: Cambridge University Press, 1997.

Willimon, William. *Acts.* Edited by James Luther Mays. Interpretation. Atlanta: John Knox, 1988.

Winter, Bruce W. "Philodemus and Paul on Rhetorical Delivery." In *Philodemus and the New Testament World,* edited by John T. Fitzgerald, Dirk Obbink, and Glenn S. Holland, 323–42. Supplements to Novum Testamentum 111. Boston: Brill, 2004.

Wire, Antoinette Clark. *The Case for Mark Composed in Performance.* Biblical Performance Criticism 3. Eugene, OR: Cascade, 2011.

Witherington III, Ben. *The Acts of the Apostles: a Socio-Rhetorical Commentary.* Grand Rapids: Eerdmans, 1998.

———. *Matthew.* Edited by R. Scott Nash and Richard B. Vinson. Smyth and Helwys Bible Commentary. Macon, GA: Smyth and Helwys, 2006.

———. *New Testament Rhetoric: An Introductory Guide to the Art of Persuasion in and of the New Testament.* Eugene, OR: Cascade, 2009.

———. *A Socio-Rhetorical Commentary on Hebrews, James, and Jude.* Vol. 2 of *Letters and Homilies for Jewish Christians.* Downers Grove, IL: IVP Academic, 2007.

———. *A Socio-Rhetorical Commentary on Titus, 1-2 Timothy and 1-3 John.* Vol. 1 of *Letters and Homilies for Hellenized Christians.* Downers Grove, IL: IVP Academic, 2006.

Wohlegmuth, Joel R. "Entrusted Money (Matt. 25:14-28)." In *Jesus and His Parables: Interpreting the Parables of Jesus Today,* edited by V. George Shillington, 103–20. Edinburgh: T. & T. Clark, 1997.

Worthington, Ian, editor. *Voice into Text: Orality and Literacy in Ancient Greece.* Mnemosyne, Bibliotheca Classica Batava 157. New York: Brill, 1996.

Xenophon. *Oeconomicus: A Social and Historical Commentary.* Edited by Sarah B. Pomeroy. Oxford: Clarendon, 1994.

Yates, Frances A. *The Art of Memory.* Chicago: University of Chicago Press, 1966.

Subject Index

Modern Author Index

Ancient Documents Index

GRECO-ROMAN WRITINGS

Plutarch De gloria
Atheniensium

Plutarch De Iside et Osiride

Plutarch De liberis educandis

Plutarch De recta ratione
audiendi

Plutarch Moralia

Plutarch Pericles

Plutarch Quomodo adulator ab
amico internoscatur

Porphyry Vita Plotini

Quintilian Institutio Oratoria

EARLY CHRISTIAN WRITINGS